D0040681

STRANGE EVENTS

AMAZING STORIES

STRANGE EVENTS

Incredible Canadian Monsters, Curses,
Ghosts, and Other Tales

MYSTERY/HISTORY
by Johanna Bertin

To my mother, Eleonora Bertin

PUBLISHED BY ALTITUDE PUBLISHING CANADA LTD.
1500 Railway Avenue, Canmore, Alberta T1W 1P6
www.altitudepublishing.com
1-800-957-6888

Copyright 2003 © Johanna Bertin
All rights reserved
First published 2003

Extreme care has been taken to ensure that all information presented in
this book is accurate and up to date. Neither the author nor the
publisher can be held responsible for any errors.

Publisher	Stephen Hutchings
Associate Publisher	Kara Turner
Editor	Jill Foran
Digital Photo Colouring	Scott Manktelow

We acknowledge the financial support of the Government
of Canada through the Book Publishing Industry Development
Program (BPIDP) for our publishing activities.

Altitude GreenTree Program

Altitude Publishing will plant twice as many trees as were used
in the manufacturing of this product.

National Library of Canada Cataloguing in Publication Data

Bertin, Johanna
Strange events / Johanna Bertin.

(Amazing stories)
ISBN 1-55153-952-7

1. Curiosities and wonders--Canada. I. Title. II. Series: Amazing stories
(Canmore, Alta.)

AG243.B47 2003   001.94'0971   C2003-905475-6

An application for the trademark for Amazing Stories™
has been made and the registered trademark is pending.

Printed and bound in Canada by Friesens
2 4 6 8 9 7 5 3

Cover: Detail of the Lake Utopia Monster
from the *Canadian Illustrated News* Nov. 30, 1872

(Reproduced courtesy of The New Brunswick Museum, Saint John, N.B.)

Contents

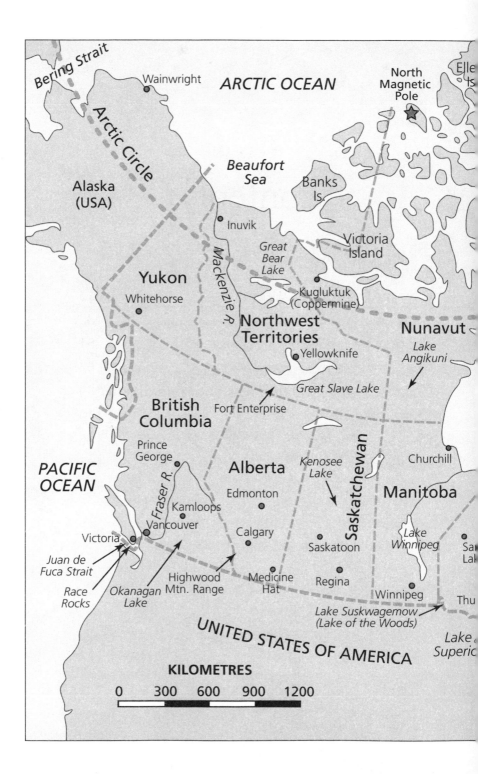

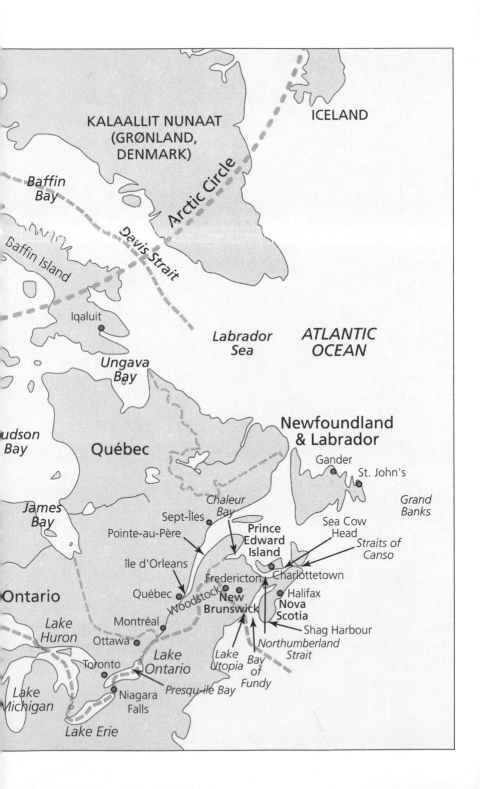

Prologue

The crew of the cargo ship Quinlan *were uneasy. Their trip across Lake Ontario had been uneventful thus far, but they couldn't dispel their feelings of dread. It was if they were waiting for something to happen, something inevitable and unpleasant.*

The weather was fair and they'd loaded the coal in good time. All they had to do was sail it across the lake to Kingston, Ontario, on the North Shore. But that was what worried them. The compass heading they were on would take them to Kingston all right, but it would take them through the devil's playground first. Odd things happened there, they'd heard. Over 20 ships had gone down in those waters that year already.

The crew's apprehension deepened when the Quinlan *tacked east and entered into a fog so thick and full of moisture that it felt like cold sweat on their faces. The temperature dropped, and it began to snow thick flakes that clung to the lines and halyards and collected on the decking. The crew knocked the snow off the rigging before it could make the ship top-heavy. But as quickly as they removed it, more gathered and clung to the already covered lines and ropes.*

The wind gusted and the waves crashed into the ship, sometimes sweeping right over the men. They clung to the rigging now, soaked through and so cold they thought they'd die right there, frozen to the mast.

The crew had given up trying to steer the Quinlan. *She was no longer in their control, her compass needle swinging wildly, her rudder not responding to their attempts to guide her. It was as if "something else" had taken hold of the ship.*

Chapter 1
Devil's Playgrounds

ost Canadians have heard of the Bermuda Triangle. Many would admit to some trepidation about flying or sailing through it. But the Bermuda Triangle is a child's wading pool compared to Canada's devil's playgrounds, where magnetic disturbances wreak havoc on navigational tools, sounds are absorbed into regions of inaudibility, and people feel called to their deaths. Three of Canada's devil's playgrounds are included here, all of them "funnel areas," where immense amounts of water pass through a relatively narrow channel and play a role in many strange events.

Niagara

At midnight on March 29, 1848, Niagara Falls ran dry. It was the silence that first alerted the townspeople. One by one, woken first by the quiet and then by the excited shouts of their neighbours, the people of Niagara Falls, Ontario, walked to the falls. The water was gone.

A southwest gale had caused the stoppage. For hours the wind had blown across Lake Erie, causing ice to jam at the mouth of the Niagara River. As more and more ice built up, the seal was complete and the water flow over the falls reduced to a trickle.

In those hours when the water ceased to flow, the people of Niagara Falls went down into the riverbed and searched amongst the rocks and boulders. While the waters of the "Great Thunderer" were held back, the people found treasure: muskets from the War of 1812, Native offerings to the Great Spirit of Niagara, and thousands of gold and silver coins. They also found human bones.

On March 31, the river began to flow again. The water level rose, and with it, the level of noise. Life went back to normal. But for those 40 hours, the townspeople had seen into the heart of Niagara's devil's playground.

The Niagara River flows for 56 kilometres between two huge bodies of water: Lake Erie and Lake Ontario. Nearly 4 million litres of water is funnelled through this narrow channel every second and, as in other funnel areas in Canada, strange things seem to occur there with a far greater frequency than would normally be expected.

The area above and below the Falls is the most haunted in Canada, populated as it is with the ghosts of the battlefields of the War of 1812; the ghosts of runaway slaves from the days when Niagara Falls was the northern terminus of the Underground Railroad; and the ghosts of the victims of the Devil's Hole.

The Devil's Hole is a cave burrowed deep into the side of the Niagara Gorge, six and a half kilometres downstream from the Falls. The Seneca believed it to be the home of the Master of Dark Spirits, a giant snake called the Evil One. They avoided the cave for fear of disturbing this monster. When French explorer Robert Cavalier de LaSalle attempted to enter the cave in 1678, his guide tried to dissuade him, warning him that no one who went in escaped unharmed. But LaSalle ignored him and entered the dark chamber. He was to pay the price. Though he emerged unscathed, Lasalle went on to experience countless difficulties during his explorations and was eventually murdered by mutineers. More deaths were to follow.

On September 14, 1763, the Seneca massacred a wagon train of settlers as they climbed the portage route above the Niagara River at Devil's Hole. Only two settlers survived: a young boy who jumped from a wagon and hid in the brush overhanging the gorge, and a British soldier named John Stedman. Stedman raced to Fort Schlosser to report the massacre. When he returned with 80 troops, the Seneca were expecting them. They slaughtered and scalped the soldiers and threw their bodies into the gorge on top of those of the settlers. The Evil One ate well.

The Devil's Hole claimed its next victim — a famous one — on September 6, 1901. United States President William McKinley visited the cave against the advice of his security guards. Hours later, he was murdered at the Pan American Exhibition in Buffalo, New York.

The Devil's Hole is just one of Niagara's many dangers. Above the Falls, the Niagara River splits into two channels. The rapids area from this split to the crest of the Falls is known as "The Deadline," a name that evokes all the tension and anxiety of an inevitable fate. Few have escaped their deaths once caught in The Deadline, where the river drops 16 metres in less than a kilometre and the waters can drag a person along at more than 40 kilometres an hour.

Danger lurks below the Falls too.

The Niagara Falls are not where they used to be. Twelve thousand years ago, they were 11 kilometres downstream. However, years of erosion have moved the falls and changed the riverbed, carving out a sharp bend and forming the Niagara Whirlpool — a whirlpool like no other.

Every day from 8:00 a.m. to 9:00 p.m., the whirlpool flows in a counter-clockwise direction. At 9:00 p.m., the water flow reverses and swirls in a clockwise direction until 8:00 a.m. the next morning. At the changeover, the whirlpool churns as the forces of the opposing waters fight against each other.

Accidents and bad luck plague the whirlpool and those who enter it. On February 12, 1906, the Whirlpool Shop and Car Barn that served the Great Gorge Route (a tourist attraction trolley car that ran along tracks at the base of the Niagara Gorge) burned to the ground. Thirteen months later, on March 12, 1907, a cascade of ice thundered down the gorge, killing a conductor and eight passengers on a Great Gorge trolley car.

Accidents continued. In 1910, two Great Gorge trolley cars crashed head-on and derailed, injuring two passengers and terrifying the rest, who barely escaped death in the whirlpool rapids. On July 15, 1915, people sought shelter from the rain on another Great Gorge trolley car. One hundred and fifty-seven people jammed into the trolley built for 84. The trolley headed down the steep escarpment on the Canadian side of the Falls, gathering momentum until it was tearing down the tracks at a furious pace. When it reached the sharp curve at the base of the slope, it derailed, rolled over, and came to rest against a tree. Passengers were flung out of the trolley, some into the water, others onto the rocky shore. The toll of casualties was 13 dead, 70 injured.

There were to be still more victims. June of 1917 was a rain-filled month. By July 1, the ground supporting the rail bed was waterlogged and showed signs of erosion. A customs officer had noticed pockets of air along the tracks where there should have been only gravel. He spoke to the rail men of the Great Gorge trolley, warning them that the rail bed looked ready to give way. They ignored his warning, and the trolleys continued to run that day. In the afternoon, the rail bed under the track collapsed, and a trolley that was filled to capacity derailed. The trolley rolled down the embankment until it landed upside down on submerged rocks in the water of the whirlpool rapids. Survivors raced to the trolley car to save the people trapped inside, but they were too late. The rush of the water flipped the trolley once more and it was swept into the torrent of the river. The gorge had claimed 12 more people.

The influence of the devil's playground of Niagara is not only felt at the Great Gorge and Falls. It extends into the adjoining lakes of Ontario and Erie as well. During the War of 1812, two American vessels — the

99-tonne *Scourge* and the 101-tonne *Hamilton* — were both lost in a bizarre accident. Returning to their mooring at Niagara, they simultaneously, and with no apparent reason, capsized, trapping their crews below deck. Only 10 of the 200 crew survived. No one could explain what happened, though some suspected that a wave possessing "the power of a battering ram" had been the cause of the tragedy. This wave would have risen up as if spawned on the lakebed deep beneath the water's surface. The sailors might have seen a slowly rising swell on a calm surface, but it would have seemed benign. Then the wave would have grown higher and higher until it overwhelmed the boats, turning them over as if they were pieces of driftwood.

The most frightening characteristic of the devil's playground of the Niagara is that it seems to beckon people to their own deaths. It is estimated that since 1850, more than 5000 people have taken their lives at Niagara Falls. But the Falls didn't always have this effect. In 1825, they were seen as a pilgrimage destination — a place where the grandeur of God and his creation could be viewed in all its magnificence. Harriet Beecher Stowe, author of the *Underground Railroad*, was one of the people who changed that. In 1836, contemplating suicide at Niagara Falls, she wrote a letter in which she stated, "I felt I could have gone over with the waters. It would be so beautiful a death; there would be no fear in it."

But she was terribly wrong. With a few very notable exceptions, those who have gone over the Falls have been found dismembered, decapitated, and disembowelled. Some have taken the plunge in desperation, but there are others who have gone over the Falls in search of thrills and glory. Retrieving them from the water has become so risky for search and rescue teams that today, the "unlawful performance of a stunt" at the Falls results in a $25,000 fine and a jail sentence.

Still, the hypnotic effect of this devil's playground continues to exert its influence. Those who have fallen under its spell (and have lived to tell about it), have suggested it was like the call of a siren, "drawing and inviting" with so powerful a voice that they were unable to resist listening.

The Marysburgh Vortex

In the spring of 1804, Captain Charles Selleck sailed the HMS *Lady Mary* across Lake Ontario. He was tired and eager to moor in Presqu'ile Bay, just west of Belleville, but first he had to cross the treacherous triangular area that extended out into the lake from the entrance to the bay. He hadn't had much trouble with the area himself, but he had heard tales that made him cautious: tales of ships that had disappeared, of ships that had lost their compasses.

Selleck brought the *Lady Mary* around and pointed her into the calmer waters of the bay. Suddenly, one of his crew called out to him. He had seen something on the water, something odd, as if the surface was being disturbed from beneath.

Selleck ordered that a dingy be lowered into the water. He and the crewmember rowed over to what seemed to be a rock or a shoal jutting close to the surface. The captain was surprised. Such a rock did not appear on any of his navigation charts. As they drew closer, he realized that something extraordinary had happened. The rock he was looking at measured 12 metres across. How had such an obstacle, an obvious hazard to navigation, gone undetected for so many years? Was it yet another facet of the devil's playground? He returned to the *Lady Mary* and retrieved his sounding equipment. The readings astounded him. The rock apparently went down 90 metres, yet the waters there were relatively shallow. The captain repeated the soundings at each side of the obstacle; the result was the same.

Giving the rock a wide berth, Selleck sailed into the harbour and went to report his findings to the harbourmaster. The rock was an obvious danger to any ship that drew more than 60 centimetres of water. The harbourmaster investigated. No one else had spoken of the rock and he wanted to see it for himself. He drew the same conclusion: there appeared to be a stone pillar embedded in the bottom of the lake.

Soon, the curious were heading out in rowboats, in canoes, in fishing boats. The brave ones climbed over the sides of their boats and stood on the rock, the water reaching only to their calves. That summer, Captain Thomas Paxton, one of two commanders of the government schooner the *Speedy*, was taken out to see the rock while he vacationed in the area. It was hoped that he would bring news of the pillar back to York (present-day Toronto) and perhaps prevent a tragedy. But that was not to be the case.

The *Speedy* was but one of many ships that went missing in the waters of Lake Ontario. In one year alone, more than 40 vessels and 672 lives were lost. Two-thirds of these ships went down in the eastern end of the lake, many of them in an area known as the Marysburgh Vortex — a devil's playground.

The Marysburgh Vortex is an anomaly, a triangle of water off the shore of Brighton, Ontario that continues to cause havoc for mariners to this day. On the surface, it appears calm and gives no hint of danger. But underneath the surface the currents are strong, for it is here that 482,700 square kilometres of Great Lakes watershed funnel into the St. Lawrence River. There is another quirk to the area: fluctuating magnetic disturbances cause compasses to produce false readings.

Ships cannot avoid the vortex; they have to sail through it to enter the St. Lawrence River. They also have to sail through it to enter Presqu'ile Bay, and it was to Prequ'ile Bay that the *Speedy* was heading on a Sunday morning in November of 1804. She had a full complement of passengers, many of them influential in the government of Upper Canada.

In the early 1800s, tensions between Native peoples and settlers were high as more and more settlers were granted land in areas that were once Native hunting grounds. These tensions worsened in the winter of 1804, when a trader by the name of Samuel Cozens murdered an Ojibwa called Whistling Duck at Lake Scugog, a frontier settlement north of Pesqu'ile Bay. Cozens was not charged with the murder, and it seemed to the Ojibwa as though he would go unpunished. Ogetonicut, Whistling Duck's brother, arrived at the settlement in the spring of 1804 to avenge his sibling's death. But Cozens had already fled. Ogetonicut killed a settler named John Sharp instead.

Knowing that the police would pursue him with far more diligence than they would a European trader, Ogetonicut hid with family on Ward's Island, off York. It was there that he was arrested and imprisoned. But Ogetonicut could not be tried at York; he had to be returned to the area where the offence had taken place.

The government hatched a proposal. They would hold the trial at Newcastle, Ontario. Not only was Newcastle located in the district where the killing had occurred, it was also slated to be declared a new town site. The government would handle the trial and the declaration all at once. They would simply have to transport the prisoner, the members of the court, and the necessary dignitaries to Newcastle.

They chose to travel by water, and on that cold Sunday, the HMS *Speedy* headed for Presqu'ile Bay, the closest port to Newcastle. Onboard were Ogetonicut, Judge Thomas Cochrane, a sheriff, court secretaries, and a bailiff, as well as the dignitaries who would preside over the town festivities. Captain Thomas Paxton was in command of the ship.

Helped along by a strong breeze, the HMS *Speedy* made good time to Presqu'ile. But the wind grew fierce and then seemed to attack from all directions, first filling the sails till their fabric was stretched taut, then plucking at them so they puckered and deflated. The passengers were sent below so they wouldn't be swept off the deck. The crew and captain remained above, steadying the boat as best they could. Suddenly, the

HMS *Speedy* shuddered to a halt and sank.

The next morning dawned clear and bright, but it did not bring the HMS *Speedy* to harbour as was expected. The harbourmaster wondered if Captain Paxton had chosen to ride out the storm in the lake rather than attempting to make it past the rock pillar and into the bay. Fishermen went out to search the waters; villagers combed the beach looking for survivors or debris. The Americans were notified in case the ship had been forced to seek shelter on the south shore of the lake. But there was nothing.

Searchers dragged the bay around the area of the rock pillar, fearing the HMS *Speedy* may have hit the underwater obstruction. They knew by then that there was no hope of finding survivors, but thought perhaps the rock would show some evidence of a collision — perhaps some remnant of the ship would have clung to the granite.

But the pillar was no longer there! Searchers scoured the water, crisscrossing the site to see if the pillar had toppled and broken in the battering of the storm. There was no trace of it, no pile of stones to be seen on the floor of the bay. It was as if the lakebed had swallowed the HMS *Speedy* and the pillar whole.

More search parties went out on the water. It was not only a ship and crew that had been lost, but several members of the government and virtually the entire court. The impact was far-reaching and the questions continued. How could a ship, a man-of-war no less, have disappeared without a trace? If she had hit the pillar, she should have shattered, and wreckage would have washed up onshore.

In 1974, shipwreck hunter Ed Burtt of Belleville, Ontario, set out to solve the mystery. He is still trying to solve it 29 years later. Those same magnetic disturbances that wreaked havoc for the HMS *Speedy* also hampered his quest to find the wreck.

Still, he has found significant evidence: two masts, a clay pipe, spectacles, and a flintlock pistol. Enough, he says, to warrant a return to the waters of the Marysburgh Vortex in the future.

Race Rocks

It was December 25, 1865, and George Davies and his wife Rosina were pacing back and forth in the lighthouse at Race Rocks, just off the southernmost tip of Vancouver Island, British Columbia. The couple had invited Rosina's brother, sister-in-law, and three friends to join them for Christmas dinner, and it looked like a perfect day for the one-and-a-half-kilometre crossing from the mainland. The weather was good, cloudy but calm — not like some of the weather they had seen since

George had taken on duties as keeper of the lighthouse. Rosina knew the crossing could be dangerous. (The island was called Race Rocks because of the tide race that tears past the rocky outcrop at speeds of up to eight knots.)

As she stepped outside, she was relieved to see that her guests were just six metres from the jetty. She waved to them then watched in horror as their boat got caught in the riptide and capsized, throwing the passengers into the water. Rosina and George raced down to the shore, but they had no way of rescuing their friends and relatives — the lighthouse had no boat. Race Rocks had claimed five more lives.

Within a year, it would claim one more. In the winter of 1866, George Davies fell seriously ill. For nine days, the Davies flew the Union Jack at half-mast, hoping that someone would come to assist them. No one did. Rosina Davies was made a widow on the 10th day.

Race Rocks is another devil's playground, an area feared by ships and the people who sail them. Part of the "Graveyard of the Pacific," it is a place of strong and shifting ocean currents, shoals and reefs, whirlpools and high tides. In the summer seasons, southwesterly winds travel up the Juan de Fuca Straits creating wave swells and tide surges. In the winter, the winds blow out to sea, carrying doomed ships and passengers with them.

Like the Marysburgh Vortex, the Juan de Fuca Straits act as a funnel — a narrow passage through which waters from the Pacific Ocean rush in and out past Race Rocks twice a day. But the currents and tides are only part of the dangers of this area. The shoreline is rugged volcanic rock, almost vertical in places. It offers no safe haven to ships, and no handhold to shipwrecked passengers. And then there is the fog — thick white mists that envelop both ships and land alike, hiding potential dangers until it is too late.

By the late 1800s, many ships were sailing the waters of the Juan de Fuca Straits. It was the only practical route for ships heading to Victoria, Vancouver, the Inside Passage, or Seattle. The fur trade was booming and the timber trade expanding. With the increased traffic, Race Rocks was considered more and more of a hazard. It became essential to find a way to lessen the dangers it presented.

In 1860, the British Admiralty built a lighthouse station at Race Rocks in response to concerns raised by officers of the Hudson Bay Company (HBC) who had labelled the rocks a "severe hazard to navigation." Over and over, these men of the HBC had predicted that ships would run aground if nothing was done. The Americans had already installed a light at Cape Flattery on the Washington State shore. Now the British would follow suit, but it would not be soon enough.

The light was lit on December 26, 1860 — three days too late for a 349-tonne tall ship called the SS *Nanette*. While the SS *Nanette*'s crew had been familiar with the waters of the straits, they had underestimated the force and turbulence of the currents at that time of year. When the captain had realized the danger they were in, he'd called all hands on deck and together they had raised every sail, hoping to counteract the force of the current. But the ship had been doomed. With a screech of torn timbers, she had run aground at Race Rocks, gutting herself on the reefs and undersea ridges. Though her crew had been rescued, the Rocks claimed other victims later that day.

A group of people on the mainland had witnessed the SS *Nanette* founder and had struck out for Race Rocks in a canoe. They'd hoped to salvage something of the cargo and, living on the shore as they did, had felt confident at being able to cross to Race Rocks and return. They'd managed the trip over, loaded as much as they could carry into the canoe, and then set out for the return passage to the mainland. But they'd made a fatal mistake. They'd overloaded their canoe and it capsized off Albert Head. Five men, a woman, and her 18-month-old baby had been thrown into the water and dashed upon the rocks.

Strange Events

The light that might have saved the SS *Nanette* was installed on schedule. Boat crews claimed they could see it from a distance of 29 kilometres on a clear day. But fog shrouded the area for up to 45 days a year, and the list of shipwrecks continued to grow.

On January 5, 1867, the SS *Nicholas Biddle* sank. On November 6, 1877, the *Swordfish* sank. On December 12, 1882, the SS *Rosedale* sank. The *Barnard Castle* struck Race Rocks on November 2, 1886, but limped to Bentick Island, where its crew was rescued.

In 1892, in an attempt to solve the problem, the Department of Marine and Fisheries built a steam plant with two compressed-air foghorns at Race Rocks. But as it turned out, the area had yet another peculiarity that made the foghorns virtually useless. Race Rocks is a "Zone of Silence," a "region of inaudibility." The new foghorns may have sounded, but the ship crews were unable to hear them. It was as if the Zone absorbed the sound. The Zone caused other strange things to happen, too. The earth's magnetic field has a hole in the Zone at Race Rocks. And in that hole, compasses cease to function properly.

Ships continued to founder and sink. The SS *Tees* sunk in 1896. In 1901, the *Prince Victor* went to the bottom of the straits. On March 24, 1911, an especially poignant sinking was that of the ferry *Sechelt*. The captain of the *Sechelt* had set out from Victoria Harbour in good weather. He was not expecting difficulty, but it found him when a gale blew in. So strong were the winds that the captain decided, for the safety of his passengers, to return to the shelter of the harbour. He never reached that safety, for the *Sechelt* was soon caught in a beam sea. She sank so quickly that not one of her crew or passengers escaped.

Mariners continued to complain about the foghorns. As loud as the horns were, no one heard them in time to avert a disaster. In July of 1923, the *Siberian Prince* ran aground on Race Rocks. The crew testified at the inquiry that they had been unable to hear the foghorns even though they had been less than two kilometres away when they struck the shoals.

This story was repeated on November 2, 1925, when the Holland American liner *Eemdijk* ran aground on Race Rocks. Her crew and passengers were all rescued, but the seven crew of the tug *Hope* drowned when their ship sank during the salvage operation. Race Rocks was still claiming victims.

It was 1929 before a hydrographic survey ship was assigned to look into the problem with the foghorns. The engineers and scientists aboard soon discovered that the sound waves were deflected. For 37 years, the foghorns had merely served as a false sense of security to men of the sea. But even when the foghorns at Race Rocks were raised, the rocky outcrop continued to claim its victims.

On January 23, 1950, Arthur Anderson — keeper of the Race Rocks lighthouse — climbed into his boat. He planned to cross over to the mainland to buy supplies. Neither he nor his family expected him to be gone very long. It was a trip he had made many times and he knew the waters well; knew the schedule of the tides and the direction of the currents. But Mr. Anderson never returned. A search and rescue team found his boat drifting out of the path of the race, but of him, there was no trace.

Chapter 2
Water Serpents

n 1872, the Lake Utopia Monster of New Brunswick pursued a Mi'kmaq shaman, "snapping its bloody jaws in a most horrible manner." This monster was only one of many Canadian water serpents. Across Canada, early settlers armed themselves, ready to protect their families and their livestock from the rampages — real or imagined — of their own local sea serpents and lake monsters. For a time, many people believed that every large body of water in Canada had "something" living in its depths. In some cases, there is mounting evidence that they were right.

Ogopogo

Many hundreds of years ago, a wise old Native man was murdered by a stranger said to be possessed by a devil spirit. The old man's tribe called upon the gods to avenge the death of their much-loved elder. The gods responded by turning the murderer into a serpent and placing it in Lake Okanagan under the custody of the Indian Lake Goddess. For all eternity, the only companion the serpent was to be permitted was a rattlesnake.

The lake serpent bore a resemblance to the rattlesnake, but was many times its size, measuring some 15 to 21 metres in length and 30 to 60 centimetres in diameter. Like the snake, the lake serpent was green-black in colour and moved in an undulating fashion. But unlike the rattler, the serpent's loops moved in a vertical wave rather than a horizontal one. And its head did not look like that of a snake, but instead resembled that of a horse or a goat, with a beard under the chin.

In the 1700s, the Okanakane called the serpent *N'ha-a-ailk*, or Naitaka, meaning "lake demon," and carved its likeness on the prows of their canoes. And demon it was, for the serpent terrorized the lake and its settlers, leaving blood, bones, and other pieces of its victims on the shore near Squally Point, where it lived in an underwater cave off Rattlesnake Island. An angry creature, it churned the waters into such a fury when it travelled that the waves grew high and the winds howled in the heavens.

The Okanakane knew better than to venture onto the waters of the lake without first giving Naitaka a peace offering for safe travel. One man who had failed to provide the expected gift was far from shore when Naitaka seized him and his family and took them down under the waters. Many years later, people found the remains of the man's canoe high up on the mountainside, where the demon had carried him and his family in order to devour them.

In 1860, settlers armed themselves and patrolled the shores of Lake Okanagan, ready to protect their families and their livestock from Naitaka. But their guns did little to protect the horses of John McDougall.

McDougall offered no gift before setting off across the lake with his horses to help a neighbour with his haying. He was halfway to safety, his horses swimming behind the canoe, when he suddenly felt the waters shift. Looking behind him, McDougall saw his horses disappear as if dragged from below. He leaped to the stern of the canoe and cut the lead ropes. In seconds, he would have joined his horses.

With time, Naitaka changed from a man-eating monster to the friendly, fun-loving Ogopogo, as it is called today. The monster of the past is now the darling of the present. It has gone from being an angry, hunted creature to a mascot that is protected by legislation and copyright. The story of that change is remarkable.

The transition began in 1900. One of the first to notice the difference was Ruth Richardson of Okanagan Landing. She was just 10 years old and playing on the beach when, as she recalled, "all of a sudden I heard a swish of water and it drew my attention, so I looked out on the water and here was this Ogopogo up there as big as life." Dark green in colour, the creature held its horse-like head a metre above the water.

Ruth was not initially alarmed, for she said that it "was quite a way out but very still and looking at me as though I was as big a curiosity to him as he was to me." The serpent sank back beneath the water and Ruth returned to her play. But suddenly, there came another sound of splashing water, and the creature was much closer — so close that Ruth, terrified, ran to her house.

A year later, a Mr. Lysons was fishing near Squally Point when something took hold of his hook and dragged both him and his boat halfway around the island before the line snapped. The lake serpent of old would have devoured him on the spot.

A new name helped with the serpent's transformation. In 1924, its original name was discarded in favour of "Ogopogo," a name inspired by journalist Ronald

Water Serpents

Kenvyn's parody of an English music hall tune. But, perversely, it was the threat of American hunters that finally turned the tide in favour of the Naitaka/Ogopogo.

In 1926, the *Vancouver Star* reported, "hunting parties are being organized in Washington State and California to come up and hunt the Ogopogo." Canadians were incensed and saw to it that the Americans knew they would not be welcome. Positive stories about Ogopogo began to circulate. The creature was said to have circled around a boat rather than collide with it. It was also reported to have been present at a baptismal service of the Brethren of the Gospel Hall. Ogopogo was well on its way to becoming cherished.

A second threat against the lake serpent occurred on July 18, 1950, when three men working in an apple orchard at Carris Landing shot at Ogopogo with a .22 calibre rifle. An hour after the shooting, it was seen heading north "and churning up the water as if in distress." This was too much for the people of British Columbia and they sought government protection for their lake serpent. Ogopogo was soon protected under Section 26 of the Fisheries Act. "This would seem to make it illegal to shoot the Ogopogo," said the Attorney General of British Columbia.

By the 1950s, Ogopogo was becoming a sought-after trophy for tourism; towns along the shores of Lake

Okanagan began to fight for the right to claim the creature as their own. Gilbert Seabrook, manager of a radio station in Vernon, British Columbia, initiated Act One of this new battle. In 1951, Seabrook personally copyrighted the name Ogopogo. Two years later, he transferred the copyright to the citizens of Vernon. His intent was to ensure that the community would assume responsibility for the continuing care and freedom of Ogopogo. Seabrook declared that the "lovable Ogopogo truly belongs to every man, woman and child in the Okanagan Valley."

Ogopogo fever was just beginning. While it had its detractors, most people seemed to want to believe in the existence of this possible plesiosaur, an enormous aquatic reptile said to have been extinct for 65 million years.

In 1966, the Canadian Tourist Association offered $5000 for an authentic picture of the serpent. Then, a year later, the Museum of Science and Hayden Planetarium in Boston, Massachusetts, announced that one-quarter of the "library's Sea Serpent display has been devoted to North America's cousin to the Loch Ness Monster, the Ogopogo."

But there were to be more battles over Ogopogo ahead. Kelowna, a town on the eastern shore of Lake Okanagan, wanted Ogopogo for itself. It had invested heavily in the Ogopogo mystique, maintaining an Ogopogo archive and even selling "Ogopogo embryos" to tourists. The town of Peachland responded to Kelowna and Vernon's claims. City councillor Jim Nielsen put forth a motion that "Peachland, BC is the home of Ogopogo. Other Okanagan communities ... should correctly acknowledge that Ogopogo may occasionally visit their waters but the lake creature's place of domicile is within the waters of Peachland."

In 1968, a man named Art Folden filmed what could have been Ogopogo swimming across Lake Okanagan. His movie raised enough interest in the creature that the search for Ogopogo, and the battle for its ownership, raged on. In 1983, the Kelowna Chamber of Commerce upped the ante. They offered one million dollars to the person who could "prove" the existence of Ogopogo. The offer was not an empty one. Chamber members were worried enough about having to pay up that they purchased an insurance policy from Lloyd's of London to cover the value of the reward.

The stakes were raised again in July of 1989. That summer, Ken and Clem Chaplin captured Ogopogo on film for a second time. This time, the film was sent to the National Geographic Society in Washington DC for verification. The results were inconclusive but "interesting."

Canada Post featured the Ogopogo on a stamp in

October of 1990. The interest generated by this stamp was so great that the hunt for Ogopogo became international again. But this time, the people of the Okanagan greeted the eager hunters with open arms.

Camera crews descended on Kelowna. Documentaries on the sea serpent were made and featured on shows such as *Good Morning America* and *Unsolved Mysteries.* A Japanese documentary on Ogopogo drew in 80 million viewers — and this was Japan's second movie on the subject. By the close of the 21st century, the serpent that had once churned the waters of Lake Okanagan in anger was gracing the covers of *Time* and *Newsweek.* Ogopogo had won hearts all over the world.

The Cadborosaurus

Frank Stannard was 12 years old when he shot at a sea serpent with his slingshot. The year was 1881, and young Stannard was out in his canoe with five friends. He'd brought his slingshot along, hoping to take some pot shots at the seagulls at Race Rocks. The gulls kept their distance from the canoe and its six noisy passengers, but Stannard didn't mind. He found something in the water that was far worthier of his attention.

The sea serpent appeared to be as long as five canoes. Stannard watched as the creature's dark head — a head like that of a horse but with no ears — came out of the water. The serpent raised its head higher and higher until it looked down on the canoe. Stannard loosed the stone in the sling and heard the "tink" as it hit the creature. Suddenly, he realized the enormity of his action and he yelled at his friends to paddle for shore. The sea serpent lowered itself into the water, but it did not pursue them.

Like the Ogopogo, the West Coast sea serpent has been around for many hundreds of years. The Manhousat peoples of the West Coast called it *hiyitl'iik*, or "he who moves by wriggling from side to side," and the Comox peoples of the Straits of Georgia called it *Numkse-lee kwala*, "the sea monster."

Unlike the Ogopogo, however, the West Coast creature has never been anything but friendly, even playful, towards humans. People described its most "gentle appearance," and on June 26, 1897, a prospector named Osmond Ferguson swore that "when the serpent or whatever it was saw us it turned slightly toward land to avoid the boat."

Though the creature was friendly, there was no question that it frightened people. In 1905, a Mr. Welch and a friend rowed across Johnstone Strait, off North Vancouver Island, to go trout fishing in the Adams River. They were almost a kilometre from the mouth of the river when a long neck rose up out of the water and then sank below. The men were terrified and rowed for shore. Again the serpent raised its head, and the men could see that it had gained on them. But the creature did not harm them, and once they were a distance from the fishing grounds, it turned away.

Despite the sea serpent's friendliness, some people seemed bent on harming it. In July of 1917, a man called R.M. Elliott was working on a telegraph line near Port Renfrew when he observed the serpent swimming along the strait and "scrutinizing" him. Elliott, for reasons known only to him, ran to his shack, got his rifle, and shot the serpent. It was apparent that he had injured the creature, for as Elliot later recalled, "it jumped, exposing its neck length to fifteen or sixteen feet, and lashed the water to such an extent that it reminded me of a steamer docking when a kick-back or ahead is ordered."

On October 5, 1933, the West Coast sea serpent shot from relative obscurity to front-page news. That day, the *Victoria Daily Times* headline read: "Yachtsmen Tell of Huge Serpent off Victoria." The story, which shared the front page with articles about the Spanish Civil War and Japan's invasion of China, went on to read: "A giant sea serpent described as being nearly 80 feet long and about as wide as the average automobile, was seen last Sunday near Christmas Island."

How was it that sightings of a sea serpent could

compete with wars on the front page of a credible provincial newspaper? For starters, these yachtsmen witnesses were no slouches. One of them was F.W. Kemp, an official of the Provincial Library in Victoria. The other was Major W.H. Langley, Clerk of the BC Legislative Assembly, as well as a barrister and a hobby marine biologist.

Though occurring at different times and locations, these men's sightings were credible and remarkably similar. Both men had seen a serpent that they estimated to be 24 metres long and 127 centimetres in circumference. The coils of the body were raised high enough out of the water that the witnesses could see light under them. They both remarked on the incredible speed with which the creature moved, "making a great wash of white foam." So heavy was the wash that Kemp had originally mistaken the serpent for the riptide travelling down the Gulf.

The 1930s were a time of intense competition between newspapers in Victoria. While the *Victoria Daily Times* supported the existence of the sea serpent and published daily reports of sightings, the *Victoria Daily Colonist* dismissed those articles as a publicity stunt. Archie Wills, managing editor of the *Times* was insulted. His integrity as a journalist was being questioned. So, to counteract the claims, he decided he would only publish those statements that were signed and witnessed. He was thrilled with the stature of his first two witnesses; it would be hard to impeach the statements of either man.

On October 6, 1933, the much respected *New York Herald Tribune* picked up the story of the Kemp and Langley sightings. The *Vancouver Sun* joined the fray, reporting, "whole continent intrigued" by the existence of the sea serpent. That was all Wills needed. Buoyed by this show of faith, the *Victoria Daily Times* announced on October 7, 1933, "There is abundant unimpeachable evidence that some strange marine monster either has its home in the Gulf of Georgia or frequently visits those waters. The detailed reports of responsible citizens of what they have seen of the stranger and its activities transfers it from the world of fiction to that of reality."

Each morning, Wills featured the sea serpent in the pages of his paper. Not only did he solicit other reports of sightings, he also invited readers to suggest a name for the creature. On Oct 11, 1933, he received a letter suggesting the name "Cadborosaurus." The moniker was fitting, for it was in Cadboro Bay, on the southeast shore of Vancouver Island, that the creature had first been seen. The letter was signed I. Vacedun, and its return address was the local jail.

The *Victoria Daily Colonist* wasn't ready to give up

the battle yet. On October 12, it featured on its cover a picture of dolphins stranded on a California beach. The insinuation was clear: the sea serpent viewings were merely a case of mistaken identity.

Archie Wills shot back, "Any fool can disbelieve in sea serpents." Two days later, the *Victoria Daily Colonist* suggested that the sea serpent might be a conger eel. But by October 15, the *Colonist* had bought into the mystique of the sea serpent and scooped its rival with a new sighting in Cadboro Bay.

All of North America seemed intrigued with the Cadborosaurus, and people soon nicknamed it "Caddy." The nickname was appropriate; the sea serpent had a mischievous side and was known to snatch seagulls out of the air. More than one hunter lost a felled duck to its appetite.

In December of 1933, just such an event took place on South Pender Island when Cyril Andrews and Norman Georgeson were out duck hunting. "I was sitting in the front of the punt ready to pick up the bird," said Georgeson, "when about 10 feet away, out of the sea rose two coils." The coils rose six feet in the air. Attached to them was a head — a head like that of a huge horse but without ears or nostrils. As Georgeson recalled, "I was sitting only 10 feet from it, with the duck right beside the thing, when to my horror it gulped the bird down its throat. It then looked at me, its mouth wide open, and I could plainly see its teeth and tongue, which were like those on a fish."

Andrews and Georgeson did not think to give chase. But even if they had, they would never have caught the Caddy. Not only was the creature capable of swimming great distances under the surface, it also moved very fast. (In 1993, two air taxi pilots observed a Cadborosaurus travelling in excess of 65 kilometres an hour.)

If tempers once flared in newspaper offices over the existence of the Caddy, it was as nothing compared to the animosity engendered between rivals in the science community.

In 1934, the *New York Herald Tribune* featured the Caddy again after fisherman Hugo Sandstrom found a carcass on Henry Island near Prince Rupert. "Remains of Hairy Sea Serpent Silence Skeptics, Baffle Scientists," the paper trumpeted. In 1941, a second carcass was found on Kitsilano Beach in Vancouver. This one was described as having "a large horse-like head with flaring nostrils and eye sockets; a tapering snake-like body three and a half metres long, and traces of long course hair on its skin." The *Victoria Daily Times* quickly dubbed it "Sarah the Sea Hag".

Dr. Clements, professor of biology at the University of British Columbia, declared the carcass to be that of a member of the shark family. This was too much for G.V. Boorman, who shot back, "If that's a shark, I'll eat my uniform. I've seen the skeletons of scores of varieties of sharks and they had no resemblance to these remains." Having been a first aid officer at the Naden Harbour Whaling Station, Boorman was a man who knew what he was talking about. Furthermore, Boorman said he had seen a virtual twin of this carcass in 1937.

Boorman's story could not be ignored, for he had photographs to support it. He recounted how one of the whaling ships harpooned a sperm whale near Langara Island. The crew towed it back to the Naden Harbour Whaling Station, where it was flensed. Inside the stomach of the sperm whale was a creature that no one had ever seen before. The crew was comprised of a number of Asian flensers and they too were clearly excited by the unidentified animal. The body of this creature was clearly unique — so unique that Boorman took 38 photographs of the carcass.

The crew set up a table. It was too small to hold the carcass so they added packing crates at either end. They then placed a white sheet on top of the table to provide a strong contrast with their exhibit. The creature had been in the stomach of the sperm whale for at least 12 hours, and as a result, there was some damage to the skin surface.

But the evidence was clear. On the table for all to see was what Boorman called "the remains of a sperm whale's lunch: a creature of reptilian appearance 10 feet 6 inches long with animal-like vertebrae. The head has the features of a horse and the turned-down nose of a camel." Based in large part on the photographs and detailed descriptions supplied by Boorman, the Caddy was later tentatively identified as a subcategory of an extinct marine reptile known as the Crocodilian

As time passed, more Caddy carcasses were found. In December of 1947, fishermen discovered a 13-metre long carcass in Vernon Bay, Vancouver Island. This one also had a skull "closely resembling that of a horse or camel." Sixteen years later, a woman walking on Sunset Beach in Vancouver Island came across a carcass measuring seven metres in length. Though it was well along the road of decomposition, she was able to clearly recognize the horse-like features of the skull.

The consistency of the descriptions over many generations, together with the credibility of the witnesses and the evidence, lent much strength to the belief in the existence of the Cadborosaurus. When Captain Hagelund, a retired whaling captain, reported that he had captured a baby Caddy, it seemed like icing on the cake to Caddy supporters.

In August of 1968, Captain Hagelund was sailing

with his family through the Gulf Islands. He had anchored for the night at Pirate's Cove and was enjoying the quiet when he spotted a disturbance on the water. He lowered his dingy and set out to investigate with his youngest son. As they got closer they could see what looked like a sea snake, except that this one travelled with its head raised above the water, and the undulations of its body were not going sideways like a snake, but were breaking through the surface of the water. Getting closer still, Hagelund saw that this animal, unlike a snake, had large eyes, eyes that resembled those of a seal pup. Its snout was hooked.

Captain Hagelund and his son netted the animal and took it back to the yacht, where they placed it in a bucket for the night. Closer inspection showed Hagelund that the creature in the bucket bore a striking resemblance to the creature from the stomach of the sperm whale. It had the same yellow fuzz on its underside, the same flipper-like feet, the same scales on its back, and the same sharp teeth. But this one was only 40 centimetres long and less than two centimetres in diameter. More important, this one was the first live specimen ever captured.

Captain Hagelund passed a fitful night. On his boat was living proof of the existence of the Cadborosaurus. But would it survive the night? He could hear it moving in the bucket, the scrape of its teeth and flippers on the sides, the splash of its tail as it tried to escape.

Unable to sleep, Hagelund got up to check on his captive. That was his undoing. So taken was he with the bravery exhibited by the small creature as it turned towards him — whiskers standing out from its snout, teeth bared and lips drawn back — that he could not bare to risk being the cause of its death.

Writing his memoirs years later, Captain Hagelund recalled the moment when he decided not to turn his captive over to the Pacific Biological Station in Nanaimo. "If he were as rare a creature as my limited knowledge led me to believe then the miracle of him being in Pirate's Cove at all should not be undone by my impulsive capture. He should be allowed to go free, to survive if possible, and fulfill his purpose. If he were successful, we should possibly see more of his kind not less. If he perished in my hands, he would only be a forgotten curiosity."

That August night in 1968, Captain Hagelund had carried the bucket to the stern of the yacht and gently returned the young Caddy to the waters of Pirate's Cove.

Chapter 3
Wild Men

anada has been home to a generous number of sea serpents. But what is less known is the number of human-like "monsters" we have had in our waters and woods. Native peoples knew of these monsters long before European trappers and settlers arrived. In some cases, the monsters were feared and hunted; in others, people risked their lives to protect them.

The Gougou and Mermen
In 1603, a number of Mi'kmaq warned Samuel de Champlain to avoid the Isle of Miscou in Chaleur Bay, on the south side of the Gulf of St. Lawrence. Champlain

wrote that these peoples told him there was a frightful monster there, the "Gougou," who was shaped like a woman but was "most hideous, and of such size that according to them the tops of the masts of our vessel would not reach his waist ... and they say that he has often devoured and still devours many savages; these he puts when he can catch them, into a great pocket, and afterwards eats them ... that his pockets are so large that he could have put our vessel into it."

At first, Champlain did not believe the stories his Native guides told him about the Gougou. But he did listen to Captain Prevert, commander of one of his ships. Prevert insisted that while he had not actually seen the Gougou, he'd heard the creature "hissing" when he had passed near to its lair. Champlain, taking note of his commander's concern, and of the Mi'kmaq's obvious fear of the Gougou, made a wide berth around the island to avoid the creature.

The Gougou was not the only human-like creature that lived in Canadian waters. In 1656, Captain Rouleau had three ships fishing for cod in the Straits of Canso, the body of water between mainland Nova Scotia and Cape Breton Island. He and his crew had left the main ship and were fishing from dories when they noticed a disturbance on the water further out to sea. Such an odd sight it was that Rouleau and his men returned to the main ship to fetch a telescope.

Holding the telescope steady on the object in the water, Rouleau looked through the glass. He couldn't believe what he saw, so he passed the telescope to his first mate. The first mate confirmed the sighting and declared it to be a "monster with the appearance of a human being: a merman."

Rouleau was not without bravery — or curiosity. He decided to capture the merman. He assigned some of his crew to one of the dories. They were to distract the merman while the captain and other members of his crew rowed out beyond the monster to approach him from behind. Rouleau managed to sneak up on the merman and throw a loop over his head. But before he could tighten it, the creature dove down under the water's surface.

Rouleau remained in place on the water, hoping to capture the merman when he came up for air. But the creature had travelled far underwater. When he did surface, he was out of reach of the slow and clumsy dory. With apparent calm, the merman remained floating in the water, watching Rouleau from a safe distance. Then finally, he brushed the hair back from his eyes with webbed hands and dove beneath the waves once more.

More than 100 years later, and thousands of kilometres to the west of the Straits of Canso, a similar drama was to unfold on the waters of Lake Superior. But on this occasion, the mysterious creature was far less forgiving of the actions of humans.

On May 3, 1782, Venant St. Germain, a voyageur in the employ of the North West Company, was travelling from Grand Portage to Michilimackinac when he saw a mermaid in the water near Pie Island in Lake Superior. There was nothing scary about her. In fact, St. Germain thought she looked like a young child. He remarked on her brilliant eyes, small nose, and woolly hair. She didn't appear to be afraid of him or his party of men, but simply looked at them with a mixture of uneasiness and curiosity. St. Germain watched her for three or four minutes, and then decided to shoot her.

The voyageur picked up his rifle and drew a bead on the childlike figure in the water. But he was prevented from harming her. A Native woman, by all accounts St. Germain's companion, leaped at the voyageur and wrestled the gun from him. As the couple struggled, the mermaid submerged under the water and disappeared.

The Native woman was outraged that St. Germain would try to harm the "God of the Waters and Lakes." She prophesied that they would all perish; that they would be dashed to pieces in the expected storm. Afraid for her own life, she gathered her belongings and clambered up the steep cliffs from the shore. St. Germain paid no attention to her warning. He considered the beliefs of the Native people to be superstitious and without credence. But he was to learn differently that night.

The voyageurs set up their tents on the shore of Lake Superior. Dusk fell early that evening and with the setting of the sun, the air grew cool. St. Germain and the others sat around the fire for a time, but the air took on an even deeper chill — a chill they had not experienced this late in the season. The men retired to their tents, but they were to get no sleep.

During the night, a violent gale blew in, picking up moisture from the lake and raining it on their shelters. The voyageurs needed all their strength to keep the tents from tearing from their bindings. But soon they realized that they were at risk of losing all their supplies and even their lives if they did not move higher up the beach. The gale was of such a force that the waves seemed to chase the men up the shore, lapping at their heels as they struggled with the weight of their now soaked belongings.

St. Germain survived the wrath of the mermaid, but the experience and terror of that night stayed with him for a long time. On November 13, 1812, a full 30 years later, he appeared before two judges of the Court of King's Bench in Montreal to swear out an affidavit as to the events of the fateful evening. It seemed that it was very important for him to be recognized as the first man to see a mermaid. St. Germain did, however, adjust his recollection of the events. In his new version of the story, he had attempted merely to seize the mermaid rather than murder her.

The Windigo

On October 6, 1821, two days after the disappearance of three voyageurs from the Franklin Coppermine Expedition in the North West Territories, an Iroquois hunter by the name of Michel Teroahauté arrived back at the camp with fresh meat to share. The three men at the camp cooked the meat then devoured it, but even in their extreme hunger, they remarked on its unusual taste. Teroahauté explained that they were eating wolf meat. He had been lucky enough to come upon a freshly killed wolf that had been gored by a caribou.

The explanation was plausible, but over the next few days the men became concerned by Teroahauté's behaviour. He was growing increasingly aggressive, and as his hostility continued to mount, the other men recalled their original suspicions. Then, when one of the men was found shot, the remaining two explorers — Dr. John Richardson and John Hepburn — knew beyond a doubt that they were in grave danger. Teroahauté insisted that the man had killed himself, but the angle of the bullet made that unlikely. Questions had made Teroahauté angry, and his behaviour became even more erratic. He refused to hunt and he threatened the men. He was also heavily armed.

The two surviving men at the camp had heard about David Thompson's experience with flesh-eating cannibals at Lake of the Woods in 1799. It had been said that a 22-year-old Native hunter had one night announced that "he must have human flesh to eat, and would have it." Members in Thompson's party had become alarmed, and the boy's father had been forced to strangle his son.

Teroahauté's companions were aware of the Native belief that once a man had tasted human flesh, he developed a craving for it and could be satisfied with nothing else. Eventually this man would "turn Windigo" and be a danger to all the people of his village.

A full Windigo is frightful to behold. More than five times the height of a person, it is so thin that it cannot be seen if standing sideways. Its eyes glow red, its fangs are long and yellow, and its tongue is like that of a snake. The Windigo is not just a creature of the forest, for the Windigo starts off human. It is its lust for human meat that turns it into its animal form.

When Terouhauté returned to camp one day, Dr. Richardson, expedition surgeon and physician, shot him. Richardson believed that Terouhauté had begun to turn Windigo.

Close to 100 years later, the stage was being set in northwestern Ontario for another Windigo killing. The fur traders had long ago killed off the beaver, caribou, and even groundhog, and by the close of the 19th century, the land of the Cree peoples of Sandy Lake was empty of game. Those who could find rabbits ate the entire animal, "hair, guts and all." They ate wakwun, a black moss that grows on the rocks. They also ate the hard bits of pinecone that usually only the partridge would eat.

By 1906, food was so scarce that the people of the Sucker clan were reduced to gnawing on skins to survive. They were too weak to hunt. Already starving, the people of the village had also been hit with the flu. So, when a young woman named Wahsakapeequay became delirious and raved, when she tossed and turned and called out to her mother to ask that she be killed, to be put out of her misery, shaman Jack Fiddler sought direction from his dreams and visions. When he came out of his dream trance, he knew he had to kill Wahsakapeequay before she turned Windigo.

It is said that when a person starts to turn Windigo, one can hear the "sound of ice pressured, scraped and scrunched inside their body." The afflicted one draws deep breaths in preparation, and at the moment of screaming, turns Windigo. Jack Fiddler had no time to lose, for once the transition to Windigo was complete, it was irreversible.

The shaman took cotton and wrapped it around Wahsakapeequay's neck so that the string he would use to kill her would not cut into her skin. He then wrapped the string around Wahsakapeequay's neck and, while two men held her arms, tightened the string until she was strangled. The Windigo was dead. Jack Fiddler's brother Joseph took the body of Wahsakapeequay and buried it in a hole in the ground that had been lined with birchbark.

Rumour of the killing reached Commissioner Perry of the Royal North West Mounted Police (RNWMP). Perry did not share the Native belief in the Windigo; he saw the act of killing another person as murder and he was determined to " fully investigate the alleged homicide."

On May 9, 1907, constables J.A.W. O'Neill and William Cashman left for Bay River Narrows Lake. They had been directed to find evidence of the crime and lay charges if possible. By dog team they travelled into ancestral Sucker land, territory that had never seen a soldier or a settler. It was rough going, the snow up to their waist whenever they stepped off the track. The sleds tipped repeatedly, and each time this happened, the dogs had to be unharnessed in order to right the sleds.

Cashman and O'Neill met with the band council at Bay River Narrows Lake and asked if any deaths had taken place in the village. They were told of the people who had starved, and then they were told that Jack and Joseph Fiddler had destroyed the Windigo Wahsakapeequay. Two hunters, Norman and Angus Rae, had witnessed the killing.

The RNWMP officers and their witnesses headed for Caribou Lake, where they were told the Fiddler brothers could be found. Men, women, and children came out to greet the visitors and to look at them because they had never seen a European before. The people of Caribou Lake offered their hospitality to the "honourable red coat soldiers of the white people" while they waited for Jack and Joseph Fiddler to return from a hunt.

Two days later, the Fiddler brothers returned. To the horror of the community, the officers called Jack Fiddler and Joseph Fiddler into their tent and "explained to them the crime they [had] committed." The officers also informed the brothers that they would be taken to Norway House, a Hudson's Bay Company post where the RNWMP had a detachment and prisoner barracks.

But Jack Fiddler was not to be easily taken. He

called out to the soldiers "What has your Great Father to do with the Sucker people? This is the country of the Anishinapek who do as they please in their own hunting grounds. The soldiers wish to take me away and put us in their stone house but I have twenty young men who do not wish that I should go... What is to stop them killing you?"

Corporal Cashman responded, "The Great Father will never forget an insult offered to the men who wear his red coat." With that, Jack Fiddler agreed to go with the officers to Norway House, where Inspector Pelletier carried out a preliminary hearing into the death of the Windigo. Neither of the Fiddlers disputed the allegation that they had killed Wahsakapeequay. In fact, they readily admitted to killing the Windigo Wahsakapeequay. They didn't understand why they were being held captive.

Both Jack and Joseph Fiddler were charged with murder and placed in the barracks at Norway House, where they lingered for 10 weeks while waiting for a trial date to be set. Superintendent C.E Saunders was concerned at the delay. He knew that if the men were not set free, their families would starve during the upcoming winter. It was already August 20 and unless the men were let go by September 15, they would not be able to travel home until January of the next year. Certain that there was not enough evidence against the brothers to warrant a conviction, Saunders recommended that the charges be dropped.

To complicate matters, Jack Fiddler was obviously ill. He was 87 years old and appeared to be "troubled with faintness" and spells — spells in which he would lay for many hours, oblivious of attempts made to rouse him.

On September 30, 1907, after spending 101 days in captivity, Jack Fiddler walked down to a nearby river for water, took off his assumption belt, and entered the forest. His guard, Constable Wilkins, had focussed his attention on the other prisoners. It was 10 minutes before Wilkins noticed the old man had disappeared, and many hours more before they found his body. "He was lying on a rock with his sash tied in a large slip-knot 'round his neck," Wilkins described.

The constables carried Jack Fiddler's body to the police barracks, placed it in a coffin, and poured 24 pounds of salt over it to prevent decomposition. It was important to preserve the body for the upcoming inquest. Jack's brother Joseph was given a trial date: October 7, 1907. Commissioner Perry was determined to go ahead with the prosecution of the younger Fiddler brother. He alone would be charged with the murder of the Windigo Wahsakapeequay.

At the trial, it was apparent from the start that the

constables were uncomfortable with the charges. Constable Cashman, first witness for the Crown, pointed out that there were no settlers residing in the area of the Sucker clan and therefore there was no way for the clan to have been instructed in the ways of European law. But the trial went ahead regardless.

"Do you know why the woman was put to death?" asked the Crown Prosecutor.

Witness Angus Rae responded, "My wife told me that people were saying that the woman was going to turn into a cannibal." Rae also added that if Wasakapeequay had become a cannibal, she would have killed people and been a danger to the clan.

The jury retired and returned with a verdict of guilty of murder. They recommended mercy on "account of the prisoner's ignorance and superstition." But nevertheless, Commissioner Perry sentenced Joseph to "be hanged by the neck until [he is] dead" and sent him to the Manitoba Penitentiary at Stony Mountain to await execution.

Two weeks later, Commissioner Perry reversed his decision. It was suspected that, having obtained a conviction under European law, he felt he had made his point and could now afford to bow to the increasing pressure for leniency. In his reversal statement, Perry said that Joseph Fiddler believed "that insane persons were dangerous to the well-being of his tribe and that unless they were strangled they would turn into cannibals … it is clear that it has been the custom of the tribe from time immemorial to put to death members of their band, and other bands, who were thought by them to be insane or incurable."

Joseph Fiddler's sentence was reduced to life imprisonment. Eighteen months later, he died of consumption — just three days before the Governor General of Canada authorized his release.

Chapter 4
Curses

o one knows whether Major R. Sumerford of Vancouver, British Columbia, was cursed. He may as well have been, for between 1918 and 1930, he was struck by lightning on three occasions. After his death in 1932, lightning struck a fourth time, shattering his tombstone. Perhaps Major Sumerford was just unlucky. But the power of a curse is not to be taken lightly. There are those who believe that curses uttered in Canada have been responsible for protecting Native land from gold seekers, bringing down United States presidents, defeating the British Admiralty, and causing the worst maritime disaster in Canadian history.

The Sorcerer of Isle d'Orleans

In the summer of 1711, the French colonists of Quebec City turned to their church leaders for salvation. Invasion by the British was imminent, and Philippe de Rigaud de Vaudreuil, governor of New France, had ordered his troops to follow him to Montreal to repel an overland attack. His action left Quebec protected by little more than a volunteer militia and a population untrained in battle. Frightened, the people began to pray for divine intervention. The priests responded by conducting continuous penances and novenas. They encouraged fasting. The wealthy gave up their exterior trappings of wealth and performed charitable acts. And the nuns prayed as they embroidered sacred banners in the fervent hope of inspiring the local militia to acts of bravery.

The people of Quebec City were justified in their fear. After defeats in Europe, the British were determined to expand their empire in North America. They had amassed a huge force in Boston. Under the command of Admiral Sir Hovenden Walker were 11 warships and 60 transport ships, as well as store ships and hospital ships. Walker's army numbered 5500 soldiers, 600 sailors, and 1500 provisionals. Quebec waited and prayed.

While Admiral Walker's fleet made its way to New France, and the French colonists sought salvation through prayer, a Métis by the name of Jean Pierre Lavallée quietly went about his own preparations on the Isle d'Orleans in the St. Lawrence River. Unperturbed by talk of the looming attack, Lavallée assured his countrymen that they were not in danger. Many were inclined to believe him. After all, Lavallée was one of several peasants on Isle d'Orleans who were known and respected for their sorcery. In his 1720 *Journal Historique*, Jesuit priest and explorer Father Charlevoix remarked on the sorcerer talents of the people of the island. "The peasants," Charlevoix wrote, "have the reputation of being rather inclined to sorcery." The priest went on to insist that these peasants could foresee events of the future, and that their visions "proved surprisingly accurate."

In early August of 1711, Lavallée set off by himself for the eastern tip of Isle d'Orleans and there, on a craggy knoll, built himself a hut. He then returned to his farm, collected a huge cauldron and some other necessary items, and transported them to the hut on the knoll. Over the next few days, he spent his daylight hours at the knoll and his evenings on his farm.

On August 15, 1711, Admiral Walker and his fleet were sighted at Anticosti Island, 700 kilometres from Quebec City at the mouth of the St. Lawrence River. That same day, though news of this sighting could not possibly have reached him, Lavallée entered his hut, locked the door, and began his sorcery. Pouring his special ingredients into the large cauldron, he began his incantations. Thick white fumes rose from the pot and seeped from the hut's chimney. For a week, Lavallée stayed in the hut brewing his mixture and speaking his spells. Through these spells, he sought to control elements of the weather.

While Lavallée toiled in his rough shelter, Admiral Walker made poor progress towards Quebec. Upon reaching Anticosti Island, Walker's fleet had met a headwind so strong that he and his men had had to take shelter in the Gaspé. For five days, the British were storm stayed. Finally, on August 21, the sixth day of waiting, they were able to set out once again. Admiral Walker was jubilant. He could smell victory on the breeze. That morning, his ships started out with favourable winds, but as the day progressed, the rain began to fall and a heavy fog drifted in. The winds died down and the mighty ships of the Admiral's fleet were becalmed. Around the same time, on Isle d'Orleans, Lavallée finished his incantations, extinguished the fire under the cauldron, and returned to his farm in the valley.

On August 22, 1711 — the very day that the British had expected to defeat Quebec City — Admiral Walker woke up to a fog so dense that neither shore nor ships could be seen. Through a series of bells and gunshots, he ordered his ships to be brought together and to face southward so that they could ride out the calm. Struggling to get his bearings in the thick, disorienting mist, Walker assumed that he and his fleet had not moved from their spot of becalming the day before. But he had failed to consider the strong currents and tides of the St. Lawrence River. Unbeknown to him, they had carried his ships 112 kilometres from their original placement on the south shore of the river towards its very dangerous north shore.

Walker's captain reported that a break in the fog had shown him a glimpse of land. Still assuming that he and the fleet were floating safely near the south shore, Walker ordered his crew to change tack. Then, as day turned into night, he retired to his cabin for some rest. But he was to get no sleep. Summoned to the deck once more, Walker noticed that the fog had lifted, and was horrified to see what it revealed; in the bright moon-light, he stared at the huge breakers crashing against the cliffs of the north shore. His men were sailing at full speed to their deaths.

Walker was able to turn his own ship and head for mid-channel, but many of his men were less fortunate. A southwest wind rose up and ship after ship was destroyed, their hulls torn open on the shoals and their bows crushed against the rock. Walker could do little but listen to the screams of his men as they struggled in the cold and treacherous water until they drowned. Eight of the 60 transports were driven ashore at Ile aux Oeufs, and 884 men lost their lives. It was a shattering end to what Admiral Walker had believed would be an easy victory.

The next day, disillusioned and disheartened at the loss of so many, the admiral held a council of war. The decision to abandon the attack on Quebec was unanimous and the fleet headed home.

When bodies and debris from the British navy disaster washed up on the rocks beneath Quebec City, it became obvious to the French colonists that Admiral Walker had been defeated. The church declared that the Blessed Virgin Mary had intervened to save her people. But the habitants of Isle d'Orleans suspected otherwise. They believed that the steam from Lavallée's malodorous brew had transformed the St. Lawrence, shrouding the river in a thick white mist so that the sailors became disoriented and lost.

When Lavallée's countrymen ran to tell him of his victory over the British, the mysterious Métis responded that he was not yet finished in his torment of Admiral Walker. The peasants wondered what more Lavallée had planned. He had defeated the greatest navy in the world, wasn't that enough? Lavallée simply repeated that there was more ill to befall the admiral.

At the time that Lavallée uttered his simple promise, Admiral Walker was far away in England. He was called to the Admiralty to explain why he had failed in his mission when nothing but victory had been anticipated. As Walker entered the Admiralty office, his flagship, the *Edgar*, blew up and sank at her berth at Portsmouth Harbour. Nearly 500 sailors were drowned and many more were injured. Admiral Walker continued to suffer humiliation. He was disgraced as a result of the hearing, stripped of his rank, and retired without a pension.

Back on the Isle d'Orleans, the legendary Jean Pierre Lavallée continued to live in peace, despite the severe penalties in place at that time for those suspected of practising witchcraft. Many believed that even the church was afraid to tackle this powerful sorcerer who, according to local folklore, had single-handedly brought down the British navy.

Tecumseh's Curse
In the time leading up to the War of 1812, Tecumseh, chief and shaman of the Shawnee, aligned himself with the British against the Americans. He judged the British to be the less avaricious of the two armies. In 1811, he appealed to the Creek Indians of Georgia for support, reasoning that with his leadership and divine provenance and their

5000 warriors, they could defeat the Americans and prevent further loss of land.

Tecumseh and his half-brother Tenskwatawa (also known as the Prophet) had spoken openly of their belief that the Native peoples needed to return to their own traditions and values if they were to survive. The siblings recognized the encroachment of settlers on their land as a danger to their traditional ways of life, and felt that only by joining into a confederacy would the First Nations succeed in driving them away.

But the Creek Indians had other loyalties, and they refused to join Tecumseh in his plan. Tecumseh was incensed. "You do not believe the Great Spirit has sent me," he declared. "You shall know. I shall stamp my foot and the earth will tremble."

Soon after this declaration, on December 16, 1811, an earthquake shook an area of 2.5 million square kilometres. Journals of the time described how the ground rose and fell, the trees bent until their branches intertwined, and deep fissures gaped open in the ground. Landslides swept rocks and earth into the valleys below, and waves on the Mississippi River swamped many boats and swept others onto its banks.

For those who knew of Tecumseh's rage over the Creek Indians' refusal to join his confederacy, the earthquake was proof of the shaman's power. People came to believe that Tecumseh could not so much foretell the future, but "make it come about through what magic no one else knows."

When Tecumseh was killed at the Battle of Thames on October 5, 1813, Tenskwatawa buried the mighty chief and then exacted a curse on his behalf. Tecumseh had died from a gunshot wound to the chest, shot at close range by Colonel Richard M. Johnson of the American army. At that time, the American army was under the command of William Henry Harrison, future president of the United States. Harrison would become the first victim of Tecumseh's curse; a curse that dictated that every "Great Chief" elected at 20-year intervals would die in office. Each death, it was foretold, would serve to remind the American people of the suffering they had inflicted on Native peoples.

William Henry Harrison was elected president of the United States in 1840. However, just as Tenskwatawa had predicted, Harrison was given little chance to govern. He fell ill after his inaugural address and died of pneumonia 32 days later. In 1860, 20 years after Harrison's election, Abraham Lincoln became the 16th president of the United States. In 1865, he was killed by an assassin's bullet during his second presidential term. Just as the curse had pledged, another Great Chief had died in office.

The next "victim" of the curse was President James A. Garfield, elected in 1880. Garfield died in September 1881, two months after being shot in the back at a Washington railroad station. Two decades later, an unruffled William McKinley ran for his second term as president, and was re-elected in 1900. Within a year, he was shot dead at the Buffalo Exposition.

President Warren G. Harding was elected in 1920. Unlike his predecessors, he did not die a violent death, but succumbed to a heart attack in 1923. Still, there were some who believed that his wife had poisoned him.

The next president rumoured to be affected by the curse was Franklin D. Roosevelt, who was starting his fourth term as president when he died in 1945 after suffering a cerebral hemorrhage. Roosevelt was believed to be a victim of Tecumseh's curse because he had been elected to his third term in 1940.

In 1963, the assassination of President John F. Kennedy, who had been elected in 1960, only reinforced belief in the strength of the curse. Ronald Reagan, elected in 1980, would have joined his fellow victims if his assassin's bullet had not missed his heart. Instead of death, Reagan suffered serious injury, perhaps putting an end to the curse, and to the demise of future "Great Chiefs."

While the curse played out over the years, the spirit of Tecumseh was not at peace. Tenskwatawa had buried his half-brother on the bank of a creek, but had told no one of the location for fear that the great chief and warrior would be dug up and taken as a trophy of war. Years later, the Shawnee returned to the Thames battlefield, intending to retrieve Tecumseh's body and transport it to Oklahoma for burial in the Shawnee Nation territory. But they were unable to find the body. The creek had overflowed many times since Tecumseh's death, and the vegetation had grown so tall that landmarks were no longer recognizable.

It wasn't until 1941 that Tecumseh's burial place along the creek bed was located. After lying for 128 years in the same resting spot, his bones were disinterred and placed in a cairn of stones on Walpole Island Indian Reserve, Ontario.

The Shawnee continue to believe that Tecumseh will return, and on that day "all Indian tribes will be united."

The Lost Lemon Mine
It was the late 1800s, and tensions were high among the members of the prospecting party in the Highwood Mountain Range of Alberta. It was big, beautiful country, but the men were focussed on only one thing: finding gold. Two prospectors in the group, Frank

Lemon and a man called Blackjack, decided to set out on their own. Blackjack was considered the best prospector in the west, and the two men figured they didn't need the others. The pair said goodbye to their main party and headed south to Tobacco Plains, following an old lodge pole trail.

As the day progressed, Lemon and Blackjack continued on beyond their original destination, panning for gold as they followed the trail up High River. They climbed down into a mountain meadow and up the other side. There, sifting through the gravel of the river bottom, they found what they were looking for. At first, there were just showings of gold, but this was more than enough to encourage the partners to keep digging.

The men took out their pickaxes and set to work. They each dug a pit, piling the dirt and rock to the side and checking it for colour. As they worked, they became increasingly excited, smelling the scent of gold and imagining the riches it would bring. They soon hit pay dirt, finding what they believed to be a rich vein.

Lemon and Blackjack each extricated a chunk of ore from their diggings. They needed evidence of their find to stake their claim. That night they celebrated, high on alcohol and dreams of untold wealth. But the talk at the campfire turned ugly and full of mistrust, and the two men argued. In a fit of rage, Lemon took his axe, swung it over his head, and brought it down with tremendous force onto Blackjack's skull.

Realizing that he had killed Blackjack, Lemon paced back and forth, overwhelmed by what he had done. He heard moans and whistles coming from the brush and, growing more and more anxious, was soon convinced that he could also hear a death rattle. He believed Blackjack's ghost was haunting him. In reality, it was something far more dangerous.

William and Daniel Bendow, two Stoney Natives, had witnessed the murder and were having fun at Lemon's expense. All night long they kept up their noise, rustling bushes, sighing, and moaning. It was too much for Lemon. At the first sign of dawn, he loaded up his packhorse and left his camp. He didn't even take the time to bury Blackjack.

After Lemon's departure, the two Stoney men headed to the reservation at Morley. They reported the events to Chief Bearspaw who, believing the gold to be evil, swore them to secrecy. Bearspaw was afraid that if the story of the gold discovery got out, the country would be overrun with settlers and the hunting would be destroyed.

While the Bendows were making their way to the chief, Lemon was hightailing it to Tobacco Plains. There he sought out Jean L'Heureux, the resident priest at the town's Roman Catholic mission. L'Heureux, it was later discovered, was not a real priest. Though he had studied for the priesthood, he had been expelled from seminary school. Lemon did not know this at the time, and he poured out his guilt to the pretended cleric.

Hearing that Lemon had not buried Blackjack, an appalled L'Heureux arranged for a Métis by the name of John McDougall to go and bury the dead prospector. Armed with a detailed map drawn by Lemon, McDougall had no trouble finding the site.

McDougall moved Blackjack's body away from the campsite and covered him with rocks. He then collected Blackjack's tools and, satisfied with the scene, returned to Tobacco Plains. But he hadn't counted on the Bendow brothers.

The Stoney men had seen the Métis intruder ride up the trail. They had been on the lookout since the murder, expecting that someone would investigate. When McDougall left the site, the Bendows removed the rocks that covered Blackjack's body and scattered them on the hillside. Then they hid the body in a crevice. It would be 14 years before Blackjack would be found and given a decent burial.

Lemon remained with L'Heureux that entire winter following the murder. During these months, nightmares plagued Lemon's sleep and visions of Blackjack's terrible injury flashed before his eyes. Despite these unsettling images, Lemon was anxious to return to the site of the slaying and claim his gold.

But over the winter, others had heard of the gold find. When spring arrived, Lemon was confronted by a group of men wanting to go with him into the hills. They weren't prepared to let him go without them, and Lemon had no choice but to lead the group to the mine.

The first part of the trip was easy. Lemon had no trouble retracing his steps. He recognized the remains of abandoned cabins and the garbage and broken tools left behind by other prospectors. But as he got closer to the killing ground, he became agitated and then confused. He raved at the men and mumbled to himself. Growing angry and suspicious, the party accused him of deliberately trying to mislead them, and they threatened him. But Lemon paid them no attention. The group had no choice but to give up their search for the mine and return to Tobacco Plains.

The following year, Father L'Heureux outfitted an expedition to search for the mystery mine. He hired John McDougall to lead them, and arranged for all the participants to meet at Crows Nest Lake. But McDougall never arrived at the designated meeting place. On his way there he had stopped at Fort Kipp — widely known as a "whiskey fort" — and drank himself to death.

It seemed as if Chief Bearspaw's belief that the gold was evil and would bring ill luck to anyone seeking it was proving to be true — but Father L'Heureux did not know that yet. Eager for riches, he mounted a second expedition to the mine the following year. Again he was foiled when forest fires made the mountain trails impassable.

Undeterred, L'Heureux mounted a fourth expedition the next spring. Still hoping to claim his gold, Lemon joined L'Heureux on this trip. But even with the influence of the priest, Lemon was unable to approach the site and once again grew delirious and had to be carried back to town.

By then, the mine had gained a reputation. As Senator Daniel Riley wrote in his 1946 account of the legendary pursuit, it was as if some "strange hoodoo seemed to haunt all who sought the lost mine." Indeed, it came as no surprise that when American rancher Lafayette French took up the quest for the mine, he fell ill just days before his departure and had to cancel his first expedition. But French — who had financed Blackjack and Lemon's original prospecting activities — was bitten by the curse and spent the next 15 years looking for the mine.

At one point, French tried to threaten William Bendow into helping him search for the mine. When that failed, he bribed him. French put 25 horses and 25 cattle in a pasture and told the Stoney that they would all be his if he helped French find the mine. The American rancher had no idea that Bendow was intimately familiar with the location of the mine. He had merely assumed that Bendow's knowledge of the area would be useful.

Bendow grudgingly agreed to help French. But on the second day of the expedition, the Stoney suddenly refused to go further. He died that night, a death attributed to Wahcondah, the evil spirit who, it was believed, punished Bendow for his intention to betray the promise he had made to Chief Bearspaw to keep the location of the mine secret.

French continued searching — his fear of the curse not as strong as his thirst for the gold. In 1912, at the end of yet another solo expedition, French came down from the Highwood Mountain Range for the winter. Although his destination was the Beddington Ranch, he sought shelter from a storm in the old cabin at Emerson Cross and decided to spend the night there. Mysteriously, the cabin caught fire and burned to the ground. Nothing remained except the chimney and the burnt remnants of logs that had stood for many years.

Lafayette French had managed to escape from the cabin, but he was terribly burned. He crawled more than three kilometres to the Beddington Ranch and collapsed. The ranch hands were able to revive French long enough to hear him whisper through burnt lips: "I know all about the Lost Lemon Mine now."

Crippen's Curse

The *Empress of Ireland* was a magnificent ship. Built at the turn of the 20th century, in the Scottish shipyards of the Fairfield Shipping and Engineering Company, she had all the safety features that the *Titanic* lacked. Though designed to serve as a mail carrier for the Canadian Pacific Railway (CPR), she had room for 1550 passengers and crew. To ensure their safety, the ship was equipped with 2200 life jackets, 16 steel lifeboats, and 24 Englehart and Berthon collapsible lifeboats. Despite these fittings, as well as sealed bulkheads and watertight compartments, the *Empress of Ireland* sank to the bottom of the St. Lawrence River on May 29, 1914. Of the *Empress*'s 1477 passengers and crew, 1012 were lost — drowned or dead of hypothermia.

Even before her tragic end, many believed that the *Empress of Ireland* was doomed to disaster. She'd already had two strikes against her — one born of seafaring superstition, the other from a curse against her captain.

Though it had long been considered unlucky and

unwise to change the name of a ship, Fairfield Shipping did just that. In 1906, the CPR had commissioned the Scottish company to build two liners for its Liverpool–Quebec mail run. These liners were to be called the *Empress of Austria* and the *Empress of Germany*. But perhaps because of the war looming on the horizon, the ships were renamed the *Empress of Ireland* and the *Empress of Britain*.

The events leading up to the curse on the *Empress of Ireland*'s captain began four years later (1910) in London, England. There, an American physician by the name of Dr. Hawley Crippen took his first step from obscurity when he poisoned, dismembered, and buried his wife Cora in the cellar of their home. He moved his mistress, Ethel Le Neve, into the house soon after, then adorned her with the fine and easily identifiable jewellery of his late wife.

Suspicious neighbours immediately recognized Cora Crippen's jewellery and contacted Scotland Yard. They reported that Cora had not been seen for some time, and that in hindsight, they could recall screams coming from the Crippen house some weeks before. Chief Inspector Walter Dew, fresh from his investigation of the last Jack the Ripper killing, was eager to prove himself to his superiors. He immediately set out to interview the physician and perform a cursory search of the house.

No useful evidence was found on Dew's first visit to the Crippen house, but his suspicions were aroused enough for him to return and take another look. On his second visit, Dew found the house empty of Dr. Crippen and Le Neve, but a thorough search of the cellar did unearth the rotting torso of Cora Crippen.

The story, with all its gory details, was welcome fodder for the newspapers. Amidst all the publicity, Crippen and Le Neve, who were laying low in Europe, purchased two tickets on the transatlantic crossing of the CPR steamship the SS *Montrose*. Crippen's plan was to escape to Quebec and then make his way home to the United States. With both his and Le Neve's photos in the newspapers, the pair realized they needed to travel in disguise. Crippen shaved off his luxuriant moustache, grew a beard, and stopped wearing his glasses. Le Neve cut her hair short and wore boy's clothing. They booked their fares under the names Mister John Robinson and Master Robinson, father and son.

The couple's disguise might have worked it if weren't for Crippen's apparent continued lack of common sense. The same overconfidence that had him drape his lover with his murdered wife's jewels led him to walk hand in hand with Le Neve on the deck of the *Montrose*. On occasion, he and "his son" were seen ducking behind a lifeboat as if in search of privacy.

Curses

Captain Henry Kendall of the SS *Montrose* was an observant man, and his interest in the Robinsons was piqued. He paid closer attention to the strange duo, noting to one of his crew that the father appeared to have a permanent mark on his nose from wearing glasses, but that he never seemed to actually sport them. The captain also noted that the father's beard growth seemed new, and that it appeared as if a moustache had recently been shaved off.

One evening, Kendall invited the father and son to dine at the captain's table and then to visit him in his quarters. It was during this visit that he noticed the young Master Robinson had let out the seams of his trousers, and that they were held together with safety pins. Kendall concluded that Master Robinson was in fact a woman, and that the Robinsons bore a remarkable resemblance to Hawley Crippen and Ethel Le Neve, whose pictures appeared so prominently in the newspapers in the ship's reading room.

Captain Kendall wired the White Star Line in London and alerted them that he had the suspects of a brutal murder on his ship. Scotland Yard responded by booking passage for Chief Inspector Dew on the speedier CP *Laurentic*. Overtaking the SS *Montrose*, Dew disembarked at Rimouski, Quebec, and waited for the slower ship to catch up. He wired Kendall to inform the captain that he would board the *Montrose* at Pointe-au-Père, a headland where river pilots customarily boarded the liners to navigate the treacherous waters of the St. Lawrence River.

On July 31, 1910, Chief Inspector Dew boarded the SS *Montrose* dressed as a river pilot. In short order, he arrested Crippen and Le Neve for the murder and dismemberment of Cora Crippen.

It is not clear when Crippen first realized the role that Captain Kendall played in his capture. Perhaps it was when, with three blasts of the ship's whistle, journalists from many of the leading papers were signalled to come aboard the SS *Montrose*. They had been waiting at Pointe-au-Père, alerted by wireless reports of the arrest that was to take place that day. Once Crippen grasped Kendall's part in his arrest, he reportedly turned to the captain and placed a curse on him, promising Kendall that he would suffer for his betrayal.

Crippen was hanged in England on November 28, 1910, and Le Neve was acquitted and returned to North America. Kendall received a reward of 200 pounds sterling from Winston Churchill, then Home Secretary of England, for his assistance in Crippen's capture. Four years later, at the age of 40, Kendall assumed command of the *Empress of Ireland*.

On May 29, 1914, the *Empress of Ireland* left

Curses

Quebec Harbour and set out for the North Atlantic. As Captain Kendall dropped the river pilot off at Pointe-au-Père, he observed the approach of the *Storstad,* a large Norwegian collier. The fog was thick and getting worse, and Kendall soon lost sight of the other ship. He quickly ordered three blasts of his ship's whistle — three blasts similar to those that had unleashed the press on Crippen and Crippen's subsequent curse on Kendall.

Waiting for confirmation that the collier had safely passed, Kendall was shocked to feel his ship list to starboard as the *Storstad* sliced into her. Loaded with coal and riding low in the water, the Norwegian ship cut into the *Empress of Ireland* both above and below the waterline, penetrating almost halfway across her beam and leaving a gash four metres wide. Water poured into the gaping hole.

The *Empress of Ireland'*s engine room took the brunt of the impact and all power and manoeuvrability was lost. The watertight doors could not be closed and the ship quickly flooded. In less than 12 minutes, the mortally wounded *Empress of Ireland* rolled onto her starboard side, flinging hundreds of passengers and crew into the frigid waters of the St. Lawrence. They clung to her sides as the mighty ship — one of the CPR's most reliable and seaworthy vessels — sank under the waves.

Survivors helped each other into the few lifeboats that had been launched before the ship went down. Relay trips were made between the *Empress of Ireland* and the *Storstad*, where survivors were offloaded and the lifeboats turned around to rescue more people. Of the 1477 passengers and crew, only one-third were brought to safety.

Captain Kendall survived the sinking of his ship, and was to survive the court of inquiry that investigated the collision. After an 11-day hearing, the court of inquiry vindicated Kendall and ruled that the *Storstad* had been responsible for the accident.

Following the inquiry, the Norwegian ship was repaired and eventually set sail again. But in 1917 she was torpedoed by a German U-boat and sunk in the mid-Atlantic, giving rise to the belief that Crippen's curse had attached itself to a new victim: Captain Anderson of the *Storstad*.

Chapter 5
Ghosts, Poltergeists, and Premonitions

t sometimes seems as though every city, town, and village in Canada has a resident ghost or two. These ghosts can be as variable as the people and places that they haunt. Over the years, ghosts have appeared after deaths or as portents of deaths to come. In Northern Canada, fear of vengeful ghosts ensures that traditions surrounding disposal of the dead are honoured. But Canada's ghosts have not always taken on a human form. Sometimes they have appeared as something quite different.

The SS *Faerie Queen*
On October 7, 1859, five clear tolls rang out from the bell

of Saint James Church in Charlottetown, Prince Edward Island. It was Friday, and there was no apparent reason for the ringing. Startled by the noise, and knowing there was no service that day, two curious parishioners hurried to the church to see what was happening.

When they arrived, the bell rang a sixth time. Suddenly, the vestry doors flung open to reveal three women dressed in white. Then, on the seventh toll, the doors slammed shut. Try as they might, the two parishioners could not pry them open. They cautiously peered through a window into the vestry in time to catch a glimpse of a woman in white climbing the stairs to the belfry.

By this time, the minister and sexton had arrived to see who was ringing the bell. They brought with them the only key to the church. The four men opened the vestry door and entered the building. There was no one there. They began the steep climb to the belfry, certain that some sort of prank was afoot. When the bell tolled an eighth time, the foursome quickened their pace up the stairs, confident that they would catch the intruder. They burst into the belfry but found it empty, the bell steady in its harness, the bell rope securely tied. The women in white had disappeared.

The men looked around in astonishment. There seemed to be no explanation for the event. The belfry had only one staircase and no room to hide. Certainly no one could have climbed out of the window.

By evening, the strange story was circulating throughout the town. The Charlottetown wharf was abuzz with it as the townspeople gathered to meet the SS *Faerie Queen*, a passenger ferry that was making her maiden run that night from Nova Scotia to Prince Edward Island. Everything and everyone crossing the Northumberland Strait had to travel by boat, and the launching of a new ferry was cause for much excitement. Three of the passengers on the SS *Faerie Queen* were women from the Saint James congregation.

It was a beautiful night and people waited happily for the ferry to appear. However, when two hours had passed and the SS *Faerie Queen* had still not arrived, the crowd grew concerned. Their concern heightened when a returning fisherman confirmed that the ferry had indeed left Pictou, Nova Scotia, on schedule. The fisherman even claimed that he had seen the boat on the waters of the Northumberland Strait.

As darkness descended, the people of Charlottetown left the wharf, many presuming that the SS *Faerie Queen* had simply returned to Pictou. After all, the night air was clear and the waters of the strait were calm; it was not the sort of weather to bring trouble to a new ship.

It wasn't until the next day that the people of

Charlottetown learned the ferry had sunk. It seemed she had gone straight to the bottom of the Northumberland Strait, for there was no trace of the boat or her passengers. Rumours began to circulate. It was learned that the SS *Faerie Queen* was not seaworthy, that she was actually an old, leaking ship painted to look new. An investigation revealed that the ferry's owners had known their boat was unsafe, and that they had been warned against taking on passengers.

Two days after the SS *Faerie Queen* went down, five survivors of the wreck were found on the Nova Scotia shore. They revealed that the captain and crew of the ship had taken to the lifeboats, abandoning the eight passengers to their fate. Only five passengers had been able to scramble onto a piece of cabin decking before the ferry had sunk beneath the waves. The three women from the congregation of Saint James had disappeared with the ship.

With this news, Charlottetown was once again abuzz. Were these eight passengers — the three drowned women of Saint James and the five survivors who lived to tell what happened to them — the people for whom the bell of Saint James had mysteriously tolled that morning three days before?

Fire Spook

In the summer of 1887, the Hoyt family of Woodstock, New Brunswick, became the victim of a "malignant fire-haunting." Surprisingly, the Hoyts weren't the first people in Canada to suffer through such a horror. Earlier that year, fires of unknown origin had plagued the owners of the Hudson Hotel in Quebec. But the sheer number of fires in the New Brunswick case earned it special mention in newspapers as far away as New York and Boston. Within a 48-hour period, 40 separate fires broke out in Reginald Hoyt's small two-story wood frame home on Victoria Street.

The first fire erupted at 11 a.m. on August 6, 1887. Hoyt was sitting in his study when the room's window shade suddenly burst into flames. Shocked into action, he ripped the shade off the wall and stamped out the fire. While looking for the source of the flames, Hoyt was called to the bedroom by the cries of his wife. She was screaming that a quilt was on fire.

Hoyt and his wife beat out that fire and then rushed downstairs to stamp out the flames in the parlour rug. Next, a child's dress hanging on a peg in the bedroom began to smoulder. Mrs. Hoyt tore the dress off the peg, dunked it into a water basin, and then threw that water on the feather bed, where flames were creeping up towards the headboard.

The Hoyts were mystified. There seemed to be no logical explanation for the fires. There were no lamps burning in the house, and the wood stove was not lit. Amazingly, the flames seemed to need no oxygen. At one point, the canvas webbing lining a lounge chair was found to be on fire. It seemed to Hoyt that the flames were coming from within the objects, as if these objects were setting themselves on fire.

As he continued to battle the flames inside his home, Hoyt heard the terrified cries of his children, who ran screaming into the house saying that a basket of clothes in the shed outside had burst into flames. Hoyt called for help. He was barely able to keep up with the outbreaks of fire. When firefighters arrived at the family home, they couldn't understand what was going on. Still, they knew they had to keep the fires under control. If the flames spread to the other wooden houses on the street, the whole downtown would go up in flames.

Curious neighbours came to see what was going on. Among them was Dr. Smith, a family physician. The doctor hypothesized that the fires were being caused by an electrical short-circuit or a gas build-up. But some of the fires had started in rooms that had their windows wide open, and others had started in the barn, where there was neither electricity nor gas.

Hoyt was overwhelmed. He was a picture-frame

dealer, not a fireman. His five children were frightened, and his two nieces, already orphaned, were beyond calming. He and his wife took the children next door to their neighbour's house. When Hoyt returned to his own home, it was to find the bed linen in the children's room ablaze.

Soon enough, journalists appeared outside the Hoyt home. James Wall, local editor of *The Carlton Sentinel*, was convinced that the fires were part of an elaborate prank until he saw a white muslin curtain inexplicably burst into flames. Rushing to the curtain, he climbed on a chair and beat out the flames with his hands. A reporter from the *Boston Globe* was next to arrive. After wandering through the charred house he wrote, "In every room partially burned garments, sheets and articles of furniture were lying around, drenched with water, and the walls and ceilings were blackened with smoke." The journalist then declared, "Only untiring vigilance has prevented the house and its contents from being burned to the ground. These fires can be traced to no human agency, and even the scientists are staggered."

After plaguing the Hoyts for two long days, the fires ceased as suddenly as they had begun. The townspeople believed the house was haunted, but remarkably enough, the Hoyts suffered no further disturbances even though they continued living there for many years.

The Ghost Train of Medicine Hat

In 1908, Bob Twohey was working as an engineer on the Lethbridge train in Alberta. One day, while coupling cars on the track near Dunmore Junction, just outside Medicine Hat, he was astounded to see the headlight of an approaching train bearing down on him. Knowing it was too late for his own escape, he yelled at his fireman, Gus Day, to leap from the engine and save himself. Day jumped, but at the moment when the other train should have hit the Lethbridge train, it instead "veered to the right and flashed past," its whistle blowing.

Twohey couldn't believe it. There was only a single track where he and Day had been, but he had seen the oncoming train with its coach windows all lit. He had even seen passengers looking out those windows, staring right at him. Twohey was so frightened by what he saw that he called in sick the next morning, and the next. The following morning he returned to work, but a month later he again felt ill and told a dispatcher that he couldn't take the run to Dunmore Junction. Jim Nicholson, an engineer on the Spokane Flyer and a friend of Twohey's, accepted the run. Fireman Gus Day agreed to accompany him.

Three kilometres outside Medicine Hat, Nicholson

was shocked when a "dazzling light and shrieking whistle" came out of nowhere and headed right for his train. Paralysed with fear, he remained at the controls and watched as the oncoming train passed harmlessly by on tracks that didn't exist. Like Twohey, Nicholson swore that the passengers in the ghost train's lighted cars had looked directly at him.

When he reached Medicine Hat, Nicholson told Twohey of his experience. Twohey was relieved. He figured that since both he and Nicholson had seen the ghost train, it wasn't a premonition of death, as he had first feared. But Twohey was wrong.

At 8:30 a.m. on July 8, 1908, the Spokane Flyer left Medicine Hat en route for Swift Current, Saskatchewan. Jim Nicholson was at the controls. Three kilometres east of the rail station, his train headed up the series of curves that would take it to the top of the embankment. The train moved slowly because of the climb, and Nicholson had time to look around at the beautiful landscape. At the top of the rise, he spotted a local farmer waving and yelling at the train. Obligingly, Nicholson and the train's fireman waved and yelled a greeting back.

The men onboard the Spokane Flyer had no way of knowing that the farmer was not just being neighbourly — he was frantically signalling them to stop, for he could see what they couldn't. Climbing steadily up the other slope of the embankment was the Lethbridge train. It was travelling towards Medicine Hat on the same track as the Flyer, but in the opposite direction.

The two trains reached the top of the embankment at the same instant, giving both engineers — Jim Nicholson and Bob Twohey — just enough time to see and recognize each other before the trains collided. The crash that ensued was so thunderous "that half the population of Medicine Hat heard it." The Lethbridge locomotive was hurled off the tracks and the contents of its baggage car were jettisoned into the fields. When the rescue team searched through the wreckage of the trains they found the bodies of seven crewmembers, including those of Twohey and Nicholson.

An inquest into the disaster ruled that Jim Nicholson of the Spokane Flyer had been at fault. It was established that Nicholson had failed to confirm that the Lethbridge train had left on time and that the track was clear. Years later, Nicholson's co-workers refuted that ruling. They said the crash was "fated to happen," that it wasn't the fault of any mortal being. They had all known about Nicholson and Twohey's sightings of the ghost train, but made no mention of these sightings during the inquest. Perhaps they were afraid that telling such an unlikely a tale would affect their employment. It wasn't until 1930, with the publication of a magazine article about a Colorado ghost train, that the story came out.

The Vanishing Village

Joe Labelle immediately sensed something strange when he entered the village on the shores of Lake Angikuni in 1930. He was 800 kilometres northwest of the port of Churchill on Hudson Bay, alone on his first trapping expedition into the District of Keewatin.

Labelle had spotted the village from some distance off — the six tents had stood out in relief on the barren landscape. Eager to take shelter, he had encouraged his sled dogs to speed up. But when he arrived at the site no one was there. In fact, it looked as though nobody had been there for a very long time. The tents were weathered, and the ground around them was clear of the everyday clutter of a lived-in community.

Searching through the tents, Labelle found evidence of hasty abandonment, but no sign of violence. In one tent were two caribou parkas and two pairs of boot leggings. In other tents he found fish and animal bones, as well as a rifle that had rusted with lack of use. Labelle also discovered an Inuit grave, with "a cairn built of stones." But the grave appeared to have been opened, and the stones were pushed to one side. Labelle found no trace of the body that had once been in the grave, and no clue as to why the grave had been desecrated.

Spooked by the abandoned village, Labelle soon left, eager to be away from the mystery of the open grave before it got dark. When he returned to The Pas, Manitoba, he told his story to journalist Emmet E. Kelleher. Kelleher recognized a good story and wrote it up under the title "Tribe Lost in Barrens Of North/ Village of Dead found by Wandering Trapper Joe Labelle." The story appeared in the November 29, 1930 edition of newspapers across North America, accompanied by three photographs, one of which showed five tepees on a barren landscape, presumably the settlement at Lake Angikuni.

Readers were enthralled and worried. The RCMP were asked to investigate the fate of the people of Lake Angikuni. The RCMP, in turn, asked trappers and Inuit hunters to report any sightings of the villagers to them.

Two months later, on January 17, 1931, Commissioner Courtland Starnes issued a press release that concluded with the words of the investigating officer, Sergeant J. Nelson. "I have made diligent enquiries from different sources but can find no foundation for this story." Nelson's report went on to state that "the disappearance of an entire community would have been reported on by both the Inuit and reliable white trappers," and that no such report had ever been received. His statement concluded with the information that Labelle's trapping licence was for the area north of Flin Flon, Manitoba, casting doubt as to whether Labelle had even travelled into the Keewatin territory.

Most damaging of all, the photograph of the "Village of the Dead" that had accompanied the newspaper article was proved to be a hoax. It turned out that the photo, which was actually of a village near Fort Churchill, had been taken by an RCMP officer by the name of Rose back in 1909. The journalist Kelleher had appropriated the photograph during an earlier visit with Rose. Labelle and Kelleher were discredited. But were they discredited for the wrong reasons?

The tale of the abandoned village predates Labelle by many hundreds of years. Labelle didn't invent the story, but he did adopt it as his own. He may have heard it in his travels, for it is a story that has been told — and continues to be told — throughout the North. His mistake was to pretend that he had a starring role.

The real story of the vanishing village is a story of a tormented spirit, a spirit who could find no peace because his body had been desecrated after death. It was the custom of the Inuit of the Northwest Territories to treat their dead with dignity. In this way, the community could ensure that the *anirniq*, or spirit, of the person was appeased and would be unlikely to seek revenge upon the living. The community first wrapped the person in caribou skins, and then placed him on the ground. Rocks were piled on the body to discourage predators from feeding on it. But in one instance, as the story goes, a village ignored the custom. When an evil old man died, the villagers hastily carried him a short distance away and abandoned his unwrapped body on the ground. They placed rocks on him but did not take the time to fully cover him.

With time, the people of the village moved away. It would be many years before a member of the community stepped onto the original village site and met the spirit. That person was a young, unnamed hunter intent on proving himself as a valued member of his community. He approached the village, hoping to find food and shelter for the night, but as he drew near, he could see that the village was abandoned.

Just as Labelle recounted in his story, this young man staked his dogs and then entered the first tent. He found tools, piles of skins, and a rusty pot. It was obvious that the people had left in great haste — the skins alone represented a season of hunting. But unlike Labelle, this hunter crawled under those skins and soon fell asleep.

But he didn't sleep for long. An insistent voice

warned him to leave, to escape the ghost while he still could. The young hunter felt the tent shake. He heard the dogs bark, and then he heard the sound of panting, as if someone was running uphill. Terrified, he crawled out of the first tent and ran to another tent further away.

In the Inuit version of the story, when the hunter looked back to the first tent, he saw that it was diffused with a green light and he heard a hissing sound, a sibilant whisper. He stayed hidden under the skins until he was sure that the creature had left. He knew that he needed to check on his dogs. Without them he would die this far from home. So, plucking up his courage, he left the tent and made a dash for the dogs. His only thought was to harness them —if they were still alive— and head for home.

The dogs were frightened and trembled when he approached them, but they stood still while he harnessed them. It was as he was tying the straps on the last dog that he noticed a scattered pile of rocks and suspected that there had once been a body "buried" there. The young man remembered the story the shaman had told him about how human souls "become inverted, hostile toward the living because taboos concerning disposal of their bodies had not been observed." He knew then that he was in the presence of one of those inverted souls.

He couldn't leave soon enough. The malevolence of

the spirit was eating away at his courage. He climbed onto the sled and signalled his dogs to head for home. It took all his strength to hang on. The dogs were going at an incredible pace, and suddenly he realized why. The ghost was chasing them. All the way back to the village, the ghost followed him, catching up then falling back. At one point, the boy felt himself give up. He was numb with fear, weak from cold and hunger, and exhausted.

But he had forgotten the strength and bravery of his dogs. With their acute sense of smell, they knew that they were nearing the village and they put on a burst of speed that carried the boy to the shaman's house. The shaman heard the yipping of the dogs and came to the door. He saw the ghost following the boy and recognized him as that of the evil old man.

The struggle between the shaman and the ghost went on for a very long time, and the shaman had to call upon the spirits to help him. The ghost was very powerful; he had much hate in him, but the shaman was victorious in the end and the green light of the ghost went out.

The story of the vanishing village is a tale told to teach Inuit children the value of custom, and to instill in them a respect for the taboos surrounding death. It serves also to illustrate the need for a community to work together and to live in harmony. Joe Labelle didn't understand that when he took the story and tried to make it his own. Certainly Kelleher added to the chicanery by stealing a photograph to support Labelle's claim. The RCMP had planned to question both men if they ever returned to The Pas. There is no record that either of them ever did.

The Poltergeist of Moose Head Inn

In 1994, Dale Orsted, owner and manager of the Moose Head Inn at Kenosee Lake, Saskatchewan, had to build himself a soundproof bedroom. But even with the soundproofing, he still has to make sure that "there is a fan going, so there's always noise. So I can't hear it." The "it" that Orsted is referring to is the Moose Head Inn's resident ghost who, for years, made such a racket that Orsted would get no sleep.

Orsted's sleepless nights began in 1990, when he bought the restaurant/nightclub in Kenosee Lake. The first hint that something was wrong came when items went missing from the nightclub. They were not items of great value — mainly ashtrays and glasses — but the totals were mounting up so Orsted changed the locks on the doors. But items continued to disappear, and then more strangely, to reappear. Lights would turn on and then off again.

But the ghost — if ghost it was — was just getting

warmed up. Not content with stealing ashtrays and flicking lights, it began to make a thunderous racket at night. To Orsted, it sounded as though someone was trying to break the door down. Police were called, but there was no evidence of damage and no clue as to what was making the racket.

Orsted installed a security camera over the bar, and although the audio segment clearly recorded the sound of cupboard doors slamming shut, the video portion showed nothing but an empty bar. This was made even more bizarre by the fact that the cupboards had been taped shut before the filming.

As more time passed, the ghost's actions became harder to ignore. The poltergeist seemed determined to get Orsted's attention, as well as the attention of the bar patrons. One night, the bar's very heavy fire doors flew open and slammed shut with no outside help. A mop pail skimmed across the dance floor like a curling rock, and the dishwasher turned on, ran for a while, and then turned off again.

In 1992, Orsted decided to renovate the Moose Head Inn. The night he laid new carpet on the restaurant's floor, he was woken by the sound of moaning coming from his office. But the office was empty and locked. At four o'clock in the morning, he was awoken again, this time by a huge crash that sounded like the "noise of impact of two cars traveling at tremendous speed." Orsted moved out the next day. It would be two years before he moved back, although he continued to run the business.

The poltergeist seemed more active when there were fewer people around, but other than that there was no pattern to its actions. In 1997, Orsted invited psychics to investigate the inn — he was determined to find some clue as to the identity of the "visitor." The psychics told him that there was not one, but three ghosts living in his inn. One was apparently a cleaning lady, the second was a 16-year-old boy, and the third was an older man. The psychics then claimed to have successfully removed two of the entities, but stated that the older man refused to leave.

Orsted doubled his efforts to learn the identity of the ghost. Most people he talked with believed it to be old Archibald Grandison, the man who had founded the inn in the 1940s. Around that time, Archibald and his wife Ethel had bought an old church hall in Kipling, Saskatchewan. After having moved the hall 50 kilometres to Kenosee Lake, they had expanded and operated it for years as a teen dance hall. Poor health had caused Archibald and Ethel to sell the Moose Head Inn in 1984, but old Archibald had loved it and people believed that he continued to watch over it.

One of the psychics stated that the ghost of Archibald had been worried about leaving his wife by herself, so Orsted offered to look after her until she died. He thought this would give the ghost some comfort. Perhaps he also hoped to get some peace and quiet himself.

No such luck. One evening in August of 1998, the lights of the inn flicked on and off. Slowly, the power outage moved from room to room until all was dark. At another time, a workman turned when he felt a hand on his shoulder only to find no one was there. Staff later heard someone whistling, and watched in amazement as lights on an unplugged cigarette machine blinked on and off.

Ethel Grandison died peacefully in 1999, but the haunting of the Moose Head Inn continued. In the summer of 2002, an employee by the name of Grant Dube was working alone in the kitchen. He turned around and bumped into a man standing right behind him. Apologizing to the old man, Dube walked around him, but when he turned back, the man had disappeared.

Orsted still hopes to track down the identity of his poltergeist. Recently, he gained a new lead when he learned of a violent death that had taken place on the inn property. A local firefighter told him that years ago, a young man had been killed right behind the building.

He had been raking the ground and was electrocuted when he touched a downed power line. Orsted now wonders if this is the man who has been haunting the inn. But if he is the ghost haunting the place, what does he want?

Chapter 6
Mystery Ships

n the early morning of October 12, 1796, a young girl looked out on the Bay of Fundy and in the pre-dawn light saw a fleet of 15 ships. The ships were not in the water; they were sailing above the surface, but they rose and fell as if they rode on the waves. Phantom ships they were, and had the girl reached out her hand, it might have slid with ease through the hull of a boat. But there have been other ships in Canada, ships of solid wood and sail, which have earned the title "mystery ship" because of unexplained events surrounding them.

The *Phantom of Northumberland Strait*

The Glengarry, Prince Edward Island couple were preparing for bed when they looked out their window, attracted by a bright glow on the horizon. It was a ship, but a ship engulfed in flames! They quickly called in an alarm and were asked the particulars: Where was the ship? What did she look like? What direction was she heading? Once the couple had provided the required information, they were told that they had seen the *Phantom of Northumberland Strait.* For an hour, the couple sat and watched as the flaming ship continued north up the straits between Prince Edward Island and Nova Scotia.

The Glengarry couple was but one of many to have seen the *Phantom of Northumberland Strait* over the last 200 years. No one knows whom the ship belongs to or where she comes from. Some speculate that she may have been a Scottish immigrant ship that went missing in the 18th century, or that she might have come from the fur trade era. Another tale suggests she was once a pirate ship that was fired upon and burned to her waterline. It is said that her treasure sits on a shoal in the straits, and that the ship cannot rest until the treasure has been restored to its hold.

The *Phantom of Northumberland Strait* was first seen in 1786 at Sea Cow Head Lighthouse, Prince

Edward Island, during a northeast gale. As the light-house keeper watched, the fully rigged ship seemed to head directly towards the cliff. Powerless to save her, the lighthouse keeper stared in horror. But just when he anticipated the tearing of her hull on the rocks, she turned into the storm and disappeared.

Many sightings of the *Phantom of Northumberland Strait* have occurred along Prince Edward Island's south shore, in an area known as Lot 7 Shore. The ship appeared to people there twice in three days, and then amazingly enough, was reported in a December 8, 1953, Associated Press dispatch as making almost nightly appearances. She seems to have no schedule, no time of year, or even time of day, when she is most likely to make herself visible.

One consistent characteristic of the phantom ship is that no one can board her. People have come close on several occasions, and in one instance, they came very close. One morning, the men and women working at Charlottetown Harbour were alarmed to hear a cry of "fire!" Such an event on the docks always calls for imme-diate action, as the wharfs are coated with highly inflammable and toxic creosote, and a fire on a ship can precipitate an explosion. The men at the harbour ran down to the water's edge and saw that a ship was in flames out in the channel.

As they looked on, it was obvious to the men onshore that the large, three-masted ship was not from their era. Where had she come from? The question paled before the need to come to her assistance. Even from their position, the men could see that the ship was doomed. She was fully engulfed in flames. But the men could also see the figures of the ship's crew as they ran frantically over the boat and her rigging trying to put out the fire.

The Charlottetown men jumped into their fishing dories and headed out to the floundering ship. They had no hope of saving the vessel, but thought perhaps they could save her crew from the water. As they gained on the ship, they could feel the heat of her flames. The men scanned the water for survivors, but could see none. All of the crew still appeared to be running back and forth on the ship. Why did they not save themselves?

Suddenly, out of nowhere, a mist rose up and engulfed the ship. The men in the dories could no longer hear the crackling of the flames, nor the groans of the ship's wood as it burned. It seemed that the mist had swallowed the ship, for when the mist dissipated, there was nothing on the surface of the water.

Years later, in 1988, the crew of a ferry crossing the Northumberland Strait reported seeing a ship in flames. The crewmembers, all men who had heard the story of the *Phantom of Northumberland Strait,* directed their radar towards the location of the sighting. None were surprised when the screen detected nothing on the water.

The *Charles Haskell*

On March 7, 1866, the *Charles Haskell* was one of 300 ships anchored together, waiting out a storm off the Grand Banks, Newfoundland. At 1:00 a.m., one of the other ships, a schooner, tore her anchor loose and was driven by hurricane force winds directly towards the *Charles Haskell.*

To avoid the impact, the crew of the *Charles Haskell* cut her anchor rope. Though she managed to evade the schooner's killing course, she was driven into a third boat, the *Andrew Jackson,* out of Salem, Massachusetts. Mortally wounded, the *Andrew Jackson* sank with all her crew. Not one was saved. Those who had been below deck were trapped. The crew above deck fared no better, tossed into the waves and run over or crushed by the other ships.

The *Charles Haskell,* though damaged, managed to make it back to St. John's, Newfoundland. It seemed a sign that the schooner had overcome her bad start. While she was still in dry dock, a man had died. He had slipped on the companionway while completing the fittings. His death by a broken neck had been quick.

Quicker still was the action of the captain, who had immediately resigned his commission, alarmed by such a bad omen.

A substitute captain was found, and the *Charles Haskell* began her career in the cod fishery. She had an uneventful career until March 7, 1866. That fateful day dawned like any other in the cod fishery, but a storm rose up and the *Charles Haskell*, dropping anchor with the ships, soon became involved in the tragic sinking of the *Andrew Jackson*.

The next spring, the *Charles Haskell* returned to the same fishing grounds. She had a good season until her seventh day there — the day she entered the area where the *Andrew Jackson* had gone down. That evening, the night watch called out an alarm and gazed in horror at the surface of the water surrounding the ship. The water seemed to be boiling! Where there had once been only waves, there were now men bobbing on the surface. Mesmerized, the crew of the *Charles Haskell* watched as 12 men, dressed in oilskins, rose out of the water and climbed over the rail onto the ship. The intruders made no noise, and though they had empty sockets instead of eyes, they baited their hooks and threw their lines overboard. When dawn approached, they put down their fishing tools, climbed back over the rails, and sank into the ocean depths.

That was the story that appeared in the *Boston Globe*. The newspaper stated that the ghostly visitors never bothered the *Charles Haskell* again. But sailors tell of a second visitation.

In this recounting, the *Charles Haskell* stayed where she was that day. Her holds were not yet full of fish and the ship could not return to harbour until they were. The crew hoped that the spectres would not be back. But they were. As the sun set, the ghost sailors rose up to the surface as they had the previous night, climbed over the rails once more, and resumed baiting and setting their lines. Again they worked until dawn and then set down their nets and climbed over the rails. But unlike the previous night, they did not sink beneath the waves. Instead, they walked on the surface of the water. The sailors of the *Charles Haskell* had guessed that the spectres were the drowned crew of the *Andrew Jackson*. They were headed in the direction of Salem, Massachusetts, from whence their ship had come.

This was not the first time a dead crew was said to have taken over the ship that was the cause of their destruction. But still, such a tale as this was not long in getting spread around. Soon, no sailor would accept work on the *Charles Haskell*. Her owners abandoned her at the St. John's town wharf. Eventually, decaying and a danger to shipping, she was reportedly towed out to sea and set ablaze.

The SS *Baychimo*

By October 3, 1931, the crew of the SS *Baychimo* had had enough of living on the boat. It was miscrably uncomfortable; the pipes had frozen and the steel cabins were impossible to heat. Realizing it would be warmer living on shore, on the ice, they made preparations to leave the ship, stranded as she was in the polar pack ice of the Beaufort Sea. The crew expected that the SS *Baychimo* would remain stuck in the ice until spring. They never dreamed that the ship would embark on a 38-year voyage without them.

The SS *Baychimo* was a cargo steamer in the service of the Hudson Bay Company. Built of solid steel in Sweden in 1914, she had a long, high prow made to withstand the force of the crushing ice pack of the North. In July of each year, she left Coleman Evans Wharf in Vancouver and headed for the Arctic Circle, loaded with supplies for the RCMP posts, church missions, and Hudson's Bay posts. Each September, she returned with her holds full of pelts for the fur trade. By 1931, she had been making this yearly pilgrimage for nine years in a row, the only ship to do it more than twice. Her predecessor, the schooner *Lady Kindersley*, had been destroyed in the polar pack.

The polar pack ice was a fearsome thing. Elisha Kent Kane, a 19th century Artic explorer, described it as a "mysterious region of terror." Floes as wide as one and a half kilometres across and weighing about two million tonnes converge upon each other, "crumpling like corrugated cardboard before the enormous pressure." Ships have no chance against a force such as this, but for many years, there was no other way to deliver goods and supplies to the communities of the North. Crews just had to make sure that they headed south in time to escape the ice's winter grip.

On July 7, 1931, the SS *Baychimo* left Vancouver with a crew of 39 under the command of Captain S.A. Cornwell. There was a festive air, the ship decked out with flags and bunting from bow to stern, the crew's family members waving and cheering from the docks. The ship left the harbour and steamed north and then east into heavy winds.

On day 14 of the journey, she experienced her first sign of trouble. The steering gear wasn't working well and the ship limped into Nome in the Aleutian Islands. Crewmembers supervised the repair work to guard against "possible bootlegging," and then, with her steering gear repaired, the SS *Baychimo* crossed the Bering Straits and ran right into a wall of polar pack ice.

It was a difficult journey, with progress measured

in metres rather than kilometres. The skipper was high in the crow's nest, peering ahead and looking for a break in the ice. When he saw one, he hollered to the second mate, who in turn ordered the engine room to steam "full ahead." The SS *Baychimo* would move forward, striking the ice and going up on top of it, until the weight of the ship's bow would crush the ice and make a passage for the ship.

Sometimes the ship would have to reverse so that she could gather momentum for her charge at the ice. Always, the progress was slow, seeming to be made slower still by the noise of the ice against the steel, which "sounds and resounds like a drum." There was no stopping for quiet — the ice would have trapped the ship in moments.

For more than a week, the ship and crew were stuck at Wainwright, Alaska. They would make progress one morning, then would be forced back by the ice the next. Inuit brought them reindeer meat and duck to supplement the canned goods on the ship. On the ninth day, the ship headed out again.

On August 11, the crew of the SS *Baychimo* looked up to see the Lindberghs fly overhead on their journey to Japan. Two days later, the ship was completely iced in, unable to move since a headwind had jammed ice against the bow. Once again, the crew had to retreat to

Wainwright. And so it went until August 20, when the wind shifted once more and the ship could finally get underway. The crew purchased more reindeer meat and set out for Herschel Island, a Hudson Bay post and RCMP Territory Headquarters.

The ship stayed at Herschel Island for three days, but not by choice. Each morning she set out, but unable to get through the ice, was forced to turn back. On the fourth day, she broke through and headed for Baillie Island, then Letty Harbour, Bernard Harbour, and Coppermine. It was in Coppermine that the crew decided to unload the remainder of their northbound cargo. The winter was closing in so fast that they did not think they could reach all their ports of call before they would need to head south.

By September 9, the crew of the SS *Baychimo* were headed home, battling ice and wind as they had on the trip north. Progress was painfully slow. The ship, relieved of her cargo, was lighter now and not as effective at breaking through the ice. By September 22, the crew had resorted to blasting in order to make headway. Then they got stuck again in the ice near Sea Horse Islands. When water froze tight around their ship, the crew took the opportunity to play football with the Inuit who had sledded in by dog team from Wainwright, 33 kilometres away.

By October 3, the men of the SS *Baychimo*, caught

in the ice during a howling blizzard, recognized that they were iced in for the winter. They began to salvage material from the ship to use in an emergency shelter onshore. As they took the tank ceilings and the spar ceiling from the holds, and gathered extra clothing and gas engines, the wind direction changed again. On October 8, the land passage to their future shelter sight was destroyed in seconds. The ice, dangerous at the best of times, was treacherous now.

Captain Cornwall made the decision to move ashore, but it would take them 21 days to complete the evacuation. The wireless operator contacted the Hudson Bay Company offices and arranged for a plane to come and transport 22 of the crew to Nome. From there, they would make their way home on the last boat out. Sixteen men, chosen for their fortitude and their ability to get along, were ordered to remain on the ice for the winter. It would be their job to guard the SS *Baychimo*, to protect the one million dollars worth of furs in her hold, and to make sure that she remained the property of the Hudson Bay Company

The crew removed the hatch covers on the SS *Baychimo* and transported them to a site 250 metres from the ship. They used them to build a square shelter, then covered the whole with snow blocks. Already it was warmer than the ship's quarters. The men then went back and forth from the ship to the hut, hauling the sleds in the naval tradition, using manpower to tow the bales of furs and the supplies necessary for six months survival in frigid temperatures. They were in no danger of starvation, for the SS *Baychimo* carried a year's supply of food as well as plenty of warm clothing. Men were assigned the tasks of hauling and cutting up driftwood, sawing up ice blocks for the drinking supply, and fuelling the gas engines that charged the batteries that powered the wireless. Despite all this labour, they had a great deal of time on their hands.

By November 18, 1931, the crew had been living in the hut for 25 days. The sun had virtually disappeared from the sky, leaving the men with only four or five hours of twilight a day. Depression set in, the "blue devils" of the North, where "the very soul of man seems to be suffocated by the oppressive gloom of the unchanging polar landscape." Tension rose from too many people sharing too little space for too long a time.

Then it began to storm in earnest. James Hay, the crew's stoker, wrote that the wind on the moving ice "made quite a noise — in fact you could hear the landscape changing." When the crew finally ventured out of the hut on November 26, it was to find a huge mound of ice, over 30 metres tall, on the spot where the ship had been. At first, the men thought the mound was the

Baychimo covered with ice, but closer inspection revealed that the ship had gone, that she had snapped her moorings.

There was no longer any need for the crew to remain at the site. They broke camp and moved their supplies 80 kilometres to Point Barrow, Alaska, where they planned to remain for the immediate future.

In mid December, two trappers sighted the SS *Baychimo* on top of the polar ice pack, 72 kilometres south of her previous position. The boat was now considered salvage, and the trappers, Ollie Morris and Charlie Adraigailak, crossed over the ice, risking their lives to retrieve the ten bales of furs still aboard. When the crew of the SS *Baychimo* later heard of this, they were in awe of the trappers' bravery. Not one of them, they declared, would have risked so hazardous a crossing. And hazardous it was. When the two trappers returned to the site to remove the last bale of furs, they arrived to find the *Baychimo* had disappeared again.

As Christmas approached, the crew of the SS *Baychimo* grew quiet thinking of family and home. Their faces were bleached to a waxy paleness, their energy low from lack of exercise and motivation. Morale was poor; lethargy reduced even the bickering. They were stuck in the North, guarding a ship that wasn't even there.

Captain Cornwell decided his men needed a boost

to their spirits. They travelled by sled to Wainwright for Christmas and returned for New Year's Eve. On January 23, they celebrated the return of the sun, but as James Hay noted in his diary that day, "the weather began to get colder, as it always does with the return of the sun." For another 20 days they lived on the ice, tending the gas engines, keeping themselves and the wireless batteries warm.

On February 12, 1932, the temperature reached –52 degrees Celsius, but the men didn't care. The plane from Nome had finally arrived to take them home. The weather had prevented the plane from coming any sooner. The pilot also had news of the *Baychimo*: the Inuit had seen her close to the Alaska shore.

But the ship did not remain there for long. By March 12, 1932, she had travelled to Herschel Island, but she soon moved on. Prospectors boarded her later that summer. They reported that she was in perfect condition and that she did not appear to have been crushed by the ice.

A year later, the SS *Baychimo* played host to 30 Inuit who boarded her seeking refuge from a storm. For 10 days the storm raged, and when it was over, only 27 of the 30 Inuit had survived to make it back to shore. In 1934, the crew of the schooner *Trader* boarded the *Baychimo* and reported back that much of the furniture and remaining cargo had been damaged. In September of the following year, she was spotted drifting off the Alaskan coast.

It was not until 1939 that anyone attempted to claim her as salvage. That year, Captain Hugh Polson and his crew climbed aboard with the intention of towing her back to port. But fate and the weather were against them, and the SS *Baychimo* disappeared once more.

She may then have become trapped in a less well-travelled route, because 19 years would pass before the next sighting. On that occasion, in 1958, Paul Brock of the *Fate* boarded her and reported finding boxed mineral samples, charts, and a rusty typewriter.

In May of 1962, Inuit saw the SS *Baychimo* floating in the Beaufort Sea. She appeared rusted but seaworthy, and was heading north. In 1969, she was sighted again, stuck in the polar pack ice between Cape and Point Barrow. By that time, the ship had survived 38 years of travelling the ice pack. The common sense theory suggests that she has since sunk, for there have been no more reports of sightings. However, the SS *Baychimo* once disappeared for 19 years during her travels, and it is possible that she still floats in the North, hidden away in one of its thousands of bays and harbours.

Chapter 7
Unidentified Flying Objects

istory books would have us believe that Canadians saw their first UFO in 1924. That was the year that the "flying saucer" made its appearance in western Canada. But Canadians have been recording sightings of UFOs since the 1600s, when the Salish drew pictographs of them on rock faces in southeastern British Columbia. Today, Chris Rutkowski of the University of Manitoba continues to record UFO sightings. In 2002, some 483 men, women, and children reported seeing something in the sky that they could not explain. That number reflects a 30 percent increase over the previous year.

Unidentified Flying Objects

Globes of Light

It was November 1792, and explorer David Thompson was hungry. He hadn't eaten all day, and his first shot had missed the beaver he'd been hunting. It was bitterly cold lying in the snow on the shore of Lake Suskwagcmow (in present-day Manitoba), but he waited, hoping the beaver would reappear.

Thompson looked out over the lake, attracted by a brilliant light in the sky — a light so big and round that it dwarfed the full moon. He watched it move towards him, heading down until it struck the river ice "with the sound of a mass of jelly." The globe broke into hundreds of pieces on impact, pieces that glowed and then went dark.

The next morning, Thompson examined the ice but could see no sign of damage. He found what remained of the globe and guessed that it must have been quite heavy. Three nights later, Thompson had a second experience with the strange globes. He was walking in the forest when a large globe "entered the woods about eight feet above the ground," knocking into branches as it travelled. It didn't appear to damage the trees; rather, pieces broke off the object. The globe was larger than the one Thompson had seen the previous evening, but it did not glow as brightly.

When Thompson examined the trees the next morning, he could find no evidence of the object's passage. Though the area's aspen trees had a character-istic whitish powder on their surface, "even the fine flour on the bark was not marked." Thompson was con-founded. He suspected that the globes were meteors, but they were unlike any meteor he had seen in Europe. They gave off no heat — of that he was certain, for they had passed close by him — and they were silent on impact.

These globes of light were to figure prominently in Canadian UFO history. In 1800, the wife of John Graves Simcoe, first Lieutenant Governor of Ontario, wrote of seeing light globes over the waters of Lake Ontario. In the years following her initial report, many others have seen the globes over the lake; the objects are always moving erratically, but at great speed. They are said to be deep orange in colour and are most often seen in the winter months, when the lake is rough and there is little chance of a boat being out on the waters. Some observers have stated that the intensity of the lights dims when planes fly overhead.

It seems that evidence of these orange globes pre-dates both David Thompson and Mrs. Simcoe's sight-ings. On a rock face overlooking Christina Lake in south-eastern British Columbia is a pictograph of a circular "flying object." Like the globes, it is reddish orange in colour. Reliable estimates of the pictograph's origin con-sider it to have been painted by the Salish peoples of

Interior British Columbia more than 300 years ago.

Sightings of the globes were especially numerous from 1975 to 1980, when the objects frequently appeared over Lake Ontario from Niagara to Oshawa, east of Toronto. One of the recorded witnesses was Harry Picken, an aeronautical engineer and a member of the Canadian Aeronautics and Space Institute. Mr. Picken was unequivocal in his belief that the lights were definitely not aircraft lights: "Aircraft do not create lights of orange colour and are not of an intensity as these lights were."

Years later, Mr. Picken still retained his confidence that the lights were not aircraft. But he upped the interest of the public when he stated that he felt the "lights moved in a positive fashion as if controlled by some form of intelligence."

Flying Saucer

On the night of February 10, 1951, U.S. Naval Reserve Lieutenant Graham Bethune was piloting a four-engine U.S. Navy Super Constellation transport plane from Iceland to Gander Air Force Base, Newfoundland. Onboard were 30 passengers; pilots, navigators, and flight engineers returning home from special duty in Europe. The flight had been uneventful, but northeast of Gander, everything changed.

Bethune looked down and saw a cluster of lights.

He was surprised; it was too early into the flight for it to be Gander, and the lights didn't resemble the street grid of Gander, anyway. He questioned his navigator, Lieutenant Alfred C. Erdman. Could they possibly be off course? Erdman checked the coordinates and responded that the lights could not belong to a town because there was no town in the area.

The pilot and navigator spoke over the plane's PA system, and the passengers, all U.S. Navy personnel, looked out the windows at the lit objects below. As they watched, all but one of the lights dimmed. The dimmed lights then moved away from the one bright object, which shot up towards the plane at what Bethune estimated to be 2700 kilometres an hour. The passengers braced for impact, but when the object came to within eight kilometres of the plane, it abruptly stopped, made a 90-degree turn, and drew abreast of them. For 94 metres it kept pace with the airplane, giving the passengers an opportunity to observe it in close proximity, if only for a short time.

The shocked navy personnel watched as the reddish-orange disc disappeared over the horizon at a speed estimated to be close to 3000 kilometres an hour. The plane's magnetic compass, which had spun wildly when the object was nearby, resumed its normal behaviour. Bethune later remarked that he was glad his plane had hydraulic rather than electrical control functions.

Bethune contacted Gander Airbase. Had they seen anything? It seemed that they had. Radar had detected "something" on the screen, but Gander air traffic control officers had been unable to communicate with it.

The transport landed at Gander and taxied to the hangars, where the men disembarked and were greeted with another surprise: U.S. Air Force Intelligence officers were there to debrief them! One by one, the crew and passengers told the officers what they had seen. They described the reddish-orange disk that had a "diameter three to four times" that of their own plane. They said the disk was about nine metres thick at its centre, and that it was "curved like a dish." Bethune, who'd had the best vantage point, said that though he had seen no motion aboard the object, he'd had a "feeling that they were being observed."

Bethune and his crew and passengers then reboarded their plane and headed to their home base at Patuxent Naval Airbase in Maryland. By then, it is unlikely that they thought they would be able to go home to their families on landing. Sure enough, they were questioned again, this time by five members of the U.S. Naval Intelligence and Air Technical Intelligence.

What was perhaps most surprising to Bethune and the others was that the questions implied ready acceptance of the credibility of their sightings. The questions weren't general in nature, but specific. The interrogators wanted detailed estimates of "size, composition, and luminosity." They asked if the object interfered with the compass or controls. And they also wanted to know if the object had appeared to be "under intelligent control."

Of course, the officers from the U.S. Defence Command were not forthcoming in answering any of the crew's questions. In response to co-pilot Peter J. Mooney's question about UFOs, the reply was "I can't answer any questions."

The men were eventually allowed to go home to their families. But, several months later, the questioning began again. This time, the interrogator was a scientist believed to be in the employ of the Central Intelligence Agency (CIA). He asked Captain Bethune the same questions, but he also had something to show the pilot.

The unnamed scientist had a portfolio of photographs in his briefcase. He showed them to Bethune and asked him if he could recognize "his" UFO among the collection. Bethune was able to do so. Again, answers were not forthcoming, but Bethune was able to get corroboration of his estimate of the speed at which the disk had travelled. Radar had confirmed his estimate of 3000 kilometres an hour. The most sophisticated aircraft at that time could travel at only 850 kilometres an hour.

Parliament Hill

On November 9, 1965, at 5:16 p.m., one-sixth of the continent of North America lost its electrical power. Thirty million people in Ontario and eight U.S. states were affected. Subways stopped, elevators hung in mid-air, and lights went out. For three hours in Canada, and longer in the United States, people learned just how much they depended on electrical power.

Media reports focussed on possible causes and possible sites of origin of the problem. But there was little media attention given to the number of credible UFO sightings that had occurred at strategic hydro installations at the time of the blackout. Those sightings had numbered more than 100.

What was known was that an "unexplained surge of power from an unknown source" had caused the system to overload and crash. Dr. James E. Macdonald, a physicist at the University of Arizona, believed that UFOs could have been that "unknown source." He stated that, "the magnetic fields accompanying UFOs can create sudden power surges in transmission lines as the craft flies overhead."

Dr. Macdonald presented his findings to the U.S. Federal Power Commission (FPC). Their response convinced him that the FPC report would ignore what he had said.

He was correct in that assumption. But what he hadn't suspected was that Canada would collaborate in the cover-up.

As it turned out, Ontario Hydro-Electric Power Commission investigators were aware of the reports of the UFO sightings. In fact, Canadian officials were exchanging information with their American counterparts. But when Ontario Hydro issued a press statement regarding the cause of the blackout, it laid the blame on a "broken relay."

Dr. Macdonald believed that the Canadian and U.S. governments had agreed that, in the interest of the national security and peace of mind of both countries, Canada would shoulder the responsibility for the breakdown. This acceptance of responsibility, Macdonald felt, was done to negate the need to disclose the involvement of UFOs in the power outage.

Four years later, an electrical power blackout occurred in Ottawa. Again the blackout seemed related to the presence of UFOs in the immediate vicinity. But this time, the blackout targeted only one specific location: the Parliament Buildings, seat of the Canadian Government.

On the evening of March 4, 1969, seven RCMP officers saw a round, bright object travelling north in the sky near the Parliament Buildings. It moved at a terrific speed, then stopped and hovered for a period of time over Hull, Quebec, before disappearing into the northwest. Alarmed, the officers called the Department of National Defence. The response surprised them. A Royal Canadian Air Force captain told them he "would not be taking any active action concerning the object."

Thirty minutes later, three more RCMP officers saw flashing red lights in the sky between 24 Sussex Drive (the Prime Minister's residence) and Government House (the home of the Governor General). The officers initially assumed the objects were aircraft, but there was no engine noise, nor was there a vapour trail. The craft moved off at a considerable speed then "shot straight down toward the Ottawa River as if on a suicide crash course." Seconds before impact, it performed a 90 degree turn and disappeared into the distance.

Over the course of four months, 12 different RCMP officers saw flashing lights in the sky. Then, on June 5, 1969, three RCMP officers and several tourists watched an object in the sky over the Parliament Buildings. For several minutes the craft gave off a brilliant array of lights; first red, then green, and finally white. As it hovered there, the buildings became dark. It was as if all the lights in the east, west, and centre blocks had been sucked into the object. The RCMP called Ontario Hydro and was told that the source of the power outage was "unknown." Had the UFOs caused the blackout?

Two years later, on July 23, 1971, Montreal and Quebec City were blacked out for three and a half hours. Hydro-Quebec reported that a lightning bolt had triggered the relays. But there had been no electrical storms in the vicinity of any of the power stations at the time. More important, the blackout had coincided, yet again, with increased UFO sightings in the vicinity.

Government Projects

Many Canadians are surprised to learn that the Government of Canada once invested heavily in the study of UFOs. On December 2, 1950, the Department of Transportation (DOT) established Project Magnet. They chose Wilbert Smith, a highly respected radio engineer, to head up the study. Smith had already done work for the government during the war, when he monitored radio waves. By 1950, he was considered an international expert in electromagnetism and telecommunications, with several inventions to his credit. Recently he had applied to use DOT laboratories and field facilities to gather high-quality UFO data.

Though the government kept their investment in the project a secret, there was really no need to. The media might ridicule the government's involvement in UFO study, but a public opinion poll in 1950 showed that 50 percent of the adult population believed that

UFOs existed and were not a natural phenomena.

What neither the government nor the people knew, though, was that Wilbert Smith had been receiving mental messages from space people since 1947. He even had a nickname for them: the "boys from topside."

Smith's assignment with Project Magnet was to determine how physics, especially magnetic principles, might account for the flight pattern of flying saucers. The government provided funding, lab facilities, equipment, and specialized personnel.

In April of 1952, the Government of Canada increased its support of the study of UFOs and established the Project Second Story Committee. UFO sightings had increased in number. The government had to accept that there was some validity to the reports — especially since a great many of them came from navy pilots. The sightings were similar: the UFOs were large and yet could fly far faster, reach higher altitudes, and were more manoeuvrable than technology of the day would permit.

In June of 1952, Smith presented his findings to the committee. He believed that flying saucers were visitors from other civilizations, and that they operated on magnetic principles. He wasn't the only scientist to believe in the existence of these visitors. As early as September 15, 1950, physicist Robert Sarbacher of the

U.S. Defence Department's Research and Development Board had told Smith that, "UFOs exist and it is pretty certain that they didn't originate on earth." Sarbacher had also informed his Canadian counterpart that UFOs were the "most classified subject in the U.S. government at the present time." Both Sarbacher and Smith had seen the photographic evidence shown to the U.S. Navy pilots after the Gander, Newfoundland sighting. They had absolutely no doubt in the existence of UFOs.

On the strength of Smith's report, the DOT established an electronic UFO surveillance station at Shirley's Bay, Ontario, in 1953, and supplied it with instruments especially adapted to detect the presence of flying saucers. The results were initially disappointing. But on August 8, 1954, at 3:01 p.m., the alarm sounded.

Something had tripped the station alarm bell! That meant that the gravimeter had detected "magnetic and gravity fluctuations in the atmosphere." Smith reported that the reading was stronger than the readings recorded when a large aircraft passed overhead. He ran outside to see what had caused the disturbance. But nature was working against him that day. The cloud ceiling was low and he had only 305 metres visibility. He could detect nothing. Regardless, Smith was adamant that "no known natural atmospheric phenomenon could account for the unusual pattern."

Smith felt vindicated and took his story to the press. The Toronto *Globe and Mail* filed a report on August 10, 1954, claiming that Smith and his Project Magnet had achieved the "world's first instrument recording" of a UFO. The Department of Transportation, embarrassed perhaps by the widespread public knowledge of its interest in UFOs (and its taxpayer-funded research), responded by cutting all funding to Shirley's Bay that same day.

On the surface, it appeared as though the government had disassociated itself from the bizarre-sounding statements of their scientist. Dr. Peter Millman, Head of Upper Atmosphere Research at the National Research Council, and former Chairman of the Project Second Story Committee, issued a statement. In it he remarked "the conclusions reached in this report are entirely those of Mr. Smith and do not represent an official opinion of either the Department of Transportation or the Second Story Committee."

The closing of Shirley's Bay did put a stop to media coverage of government involvement in UFO study. But what the media did not know until much later was that the government continued its support. The Defence Research Board built a restricted landing field near Suffield, Alberta, to provide an optimal landing pad for UFOs. The board hoped to encourage UFOs to land there because they had so far been unsuccessful in their attempts to intercept UFOs with navy jets. Fortunately, unlike their American counterparts, Canada lost no pilots in the effort.

But the government was not yet finished with its UFO flip-flop. In July of 1967, Canada's Defence Minister, Paul Hellyer, had been quoted in the *Ottawa Journal* as stating that the Suffield Air Base had been closed because "UFOs did not pose a threat to National Security." Just 11 years later, Captain Douglas Caie of the Department of Defence expressed total ignorance of the base. Not only that, but he declared, "we have no record of any such project ... from the information I have, we never had one."

Today, many of the findings of Project Magnet continue to remain "classified material." The Canadian government has released only two reports: the first detailed 25 UFO sightings in 1952; the second is the report of August 8, 1954 (Shirley's Bay). But the government does continue to tabulate UFO sightings and record them at the National Research Council's Herzberg Institute of Astrophysics in the Planetary Sciences Section. The Department of National Defence also continues to liaise with NORAD Headquarters at Colorado Springs, in the United States.

Bibliography

Berton, Pierre. *The Arctic Grail: The Quest for the North West Passage and the North Pole 1818-1909*. Toronto: McClelland and Stewart, 1988.

Bondarchuk, Yurko. *UFO Sightings, Landings and Abductions: The Documented Evidence*. New York: Methuen, 1979.

Clark, Jerome. *The UFO Encyclopedia: The Phenomenon Since the Beginning*. Detroit: Omnigraphics Inc., 1998.

*Cochrane, Hugh. *Gateway to Oblivion: The Great Lakes Bermuda Triangle*. New York: Avon Books, 1980.

*Colombo, John Robert. *Mysterious Canada: Strange Sights, Extraordinary Events and Peculiar Places*. Toronto: Doubleday, 1988.

Creighton, Helen. *Bluenose Ghosts*. Toronto: Ryerson Press, 1957.

*Dempsey, Hugh, Daniel Riley and Tom Primrose. *The Lost Lemon Mine: Greatest Mystery of the Canadian Rockies*. Calgary: Frontier Books.

*Ferguson, Ted. *Sentimental Journey: An Oral History of Train Travel in Canada*. Toronto: Doubleday, 1985.

*Fiddler, Chief Thomas and James R. Stevens. *Killing the Shamen*. Moonbeam: Penumbra Press, 1985.

*Gaal, Arlene. *Beneath the Depths*. Okanagan: Valley Review Publishing Ltd., 1976.

*Gaddis, Vincent. *Invisible Horizons: For the Millions who were Fascinated by Chariot of the Gods*. New York: Ace Books, 1965.

*Hay, James. "Baychimo". *The Beaver*. Spring, 1972.

*Lambert, R.S. *Exploring the Supernatural: The Weird in Canadian Folklore*. Toronto: McClelland and Stewart, 1955.

*Leblond, Dr. Paul H. and Dr. Edward L. Blousfield. *Cadborosaurus: Survivor from the Deep*. Victoria: Horsdal and Schubart, 1995.

*Thompson, David. *David Thompson's Narrative of His Explorations in Western Alberta, 1784-1812*, ed. J.B. Tyrrell. Toronto: Champlain Society, 1916.

Trueman, Stuart. *Tall Tales and True Tales from Down East*. Toronto: McClelland and Stewart, 1979.

Qitsualik, Rachel Attituq. "Anirniq: An Inuit Ghost Story". *Indian Country Today*, August 2002.

Watson, Julie V. *Ghost Stories and Legends of Prince Edward Island*. Toronto: Hounslow Press, 1988.

The author acknowledges that the books marked with an * are the sources for the quotes within the book.

Acknowledgments

The author wishes to acknowledge the following sources for their assistance with the manuscript: Stanton Friedman, Fredericton, N.B., for his generosity in sharing his "UFO" library; the staff of the Harriet Irving Library, University of New Brunswick, for their assistance with finding elusive microfiches; and the New Brunswick Public Library system, for their flexibility with "due back dates." For their permission to use photographs from their collection: the New Brunswick Museum, The Glenbow Archives, and the Hudson Bay Company (HBC) Archives. For sharing his personal story: Dale Orsted of the Moose Head Inn, Kenosee Lake, Saskatchewan.

A note of thanks goes out to journalists everywhere, for it is they who are, and always have been, the primary recorders of current events. Without their writings, much of Canadian history would have gone unchronicled. As well, the books of John Robert Colombo, R.S. Lambert, and Helen Creighton proved invaluable, for it was they who first noted the lack of Canadian content in history books, and set out to fill the void.

A personal thank you goes to Altitude editor Jill Foran, whose comments improved the manuscript immeasurably. And last, but not least, I want to thank my family for their unstinting encouragement, and for the countless ways in which my husband Bruce took on extra responsibilities so that I could delve into Canada's fascinating past.

About the Author

Johanna Bertin is a freelance writer who lives in Smithfield, New Brunswick. Long fascinated with the quirky and the different, her articles have appeared in magazines and newspapers across the country.

OTHER AMAZING STORIES

These titles are available wherever you buy books. If you have trouble finding the book you want, call the Altitude order desk at 1-800-957-6888, e-mail your request to: orderdesk@altitudepublishing.com or visit our Web site at www.amazingstories.ca

All titles retail for $9.95 Cdn or $7.95 US. (Prices subject to change.)

New AMAZING STORIES titles are published every month. If you would like more information, e-mail your name and mailing address to: amazingstories@altitudepublishing.com.